Priscilla's Letter

Finding the Author of the Epistle to the Hebrews

Ruth Hoppin

Priscilla's Letter

Finding the Author of the Epistle to the Hebrews

Ruth Hoppin

Christian Universities Press
San Francisco - London - Bethesda
1997

Library of Congress Cataloging-in-Publication Data

Hoppin, Ruth, 1928-
Priscilla's letter : finding the author of the Epistle to the Hebrews / Ruth Hoppin
p. cm.
Includes bibliographical references and index.
ISBN 1-57309-152-9 (alk. paper). -- ISBN 1-57309-151-0 (pbk. : alk. paper)
1. Bible. N.T. Hebrews—Authorship. 2. Priscilla, Saint, 1st cent.—Authorship. I. Title.
BS2775.2.H63 1997
227'.87066—dc21 96-52682
CIP

Editorial Inquiries:
International Scholars Publications
7831 Woodmont Avenue, #345
Bethesda, MD 20814

To order: (800) 55-PUBLISH

To Stuart,
for traveling with me into the first century
to "find Priscilla"

TABLE OF CONTENTS

ACKNOWLEDGMENTS

Scripture quotations are from the Revised Standard Version of the Bible, copyright 1946, 1952, 1971 and from the New Revised Standard Version Bible, copyright 1989 by the Division of Christian Education of the National Council of Churches of Christ in the USA, except where indicated otherwise. Used by permission.

An excerpt from Edward M. Cook, *Solving the Mysteries of the Dead Sea Scrolls*, is used by permission of Zondervan Publishing House.

Quotations from the Dead Sea Scrolls are from BURROWS ON THE DEAD SEA SCROLLS by Millar Burrows. Copyright (c) 1955 by Millar Burrows. Renewed copyright (c) 1983 by E. G. Burrows. Used by permission of Viking Penguin, a division of Penguin Books USA Inc.

Slides of the Priscilla Catacomb are reproduced with permission of Sister Maria Francesca of the Benedictine Sisters, Rome.

Photograph, courtesy of Bibliothèque Nationale de France.

FOREWORD

This book makes a major contribution to the continuing search for the anonymous early Christian author who may believably be credited with the writing of the Epistle to the Hebrews. Although the thesis of Priscillian authorship is bold, the research reflected in *Priscilla's Letter* is thorough and the scholarship meticulous. In a line-up of all the possible candidates, the weight of the evidence is shown to favor this missionary pioneer of old; faithful companion of the Apostle Paul.

Such a piece of research has all the makings for dry and tedious reading. Fortunately, this is not the case. This search for Priscilla is conducted in the form of a fascinating adventure story that takes the reader through unexpected twists and turns, all over the landscape of ancient historical, archeological and literary evidence. In the process, we are served a remarkable piece of interdisciplinary virtuosity that will make its mark on New Testament studies.

Gilbert Bilezikian
Professor Emeritus of Biblical Studies
Wheaton College

PREFACE

A quarter of a century has elapsed since publication of my first book presenting the case for Priscilla's authorship of the Epistle to the Hebrews.

Why a second book on the same topic? *Priscilla's Letter: Finding the Author of the Epistle to the Hebrews* evolved out of a strange sequence of events, as did *Priscilla: Author of the Epistle to the Hebrews.*

In the mid-1960's, while researching mistranslations of scripture pertaining to the status of women, I came across a reference to Harnack's hypothesis that Priscilla wrote Hebrews. I didn't realize it then, but a remarkable adventure had commenced. At first I pondered: "Could it possibly be true, and was there any supporting evidence?" Planning to write an article, at most, I researched a book, answering both questions affirmatively.

Throughout the 1970's, I lectured on Priscilla's authorship of Hebrews. When books were no longer available, I circulated the text of one lecture, "A Female Author of Scripture," in response to inquiries.

However, I began moving in a different direction - toward free-lance writing and poetry. Advocacy of "Priscilla's Letter" seemed to be an episode in my life - an episode that had receded into the past.

The turning point came in 1983, with a telephone call from one of my readers, Martha Sihler of Santa Cruz. Ms. Sihler was convinced that Priscilla was the author of Hebrews, and she resolved to search for additional documentation. She provided valuable new material.

Other circumstances converged, leading to a second book about Priscilla. Important new commentaries on Hebrews were published, expanding the base of knowledge. Additional Dead Sea Scrolls were published, precipitating discussion of various issues related to the book. Clearly, an update was needed.

I was invited to present a workshop on Priscilla at a conference; I saw an increase in public interest.

Most important of all, my thoughts had turned decisively towards a sequel to *Priscilla: Author of the Epistle to the Hebrews*. My research was under way.

In addition to Martha Sihler, other persons deserve grateful acknowledgment: Carolyn Goodman Plampin for information and encouragement; Cathie Scalice, Kate Harvest, Katharine Legge, and Lolly Pineda, Reference Librarians at Serramonte Library, Daly City, for their patience and helpfulness in obtaining books and articles through inter-library loan; Leonard E. Boyle of Bibliotheca Apostolica Vaticana for kindly providing a source and a Latin-English translation; Julie E. Johnson of San Francisco, French-English translator; Maureen J. Hoffmann for assistance in preparing the manuscript; Rev. Ray Munson of North Collins, N.Y. for spreading the word about Priscilla, and for inspiration and prayer; and Sister Maria Francesca of the Benedictine Sisters, Priscilla Catacomb, Rome, for a special tour of the Catacomb in 1988.

I appreciate the courteous assistance of *The Expository Times* and the Bibliothèque Nationale de France.

I want to mention with gratitude Gilbert Bilezikian and Verna J. Dozier, both of whom graciously consented to read the manuscript.

The person to whom this book is dedicated, my husband Stuart, deserves credit for his supportiveness and assistance.

In 1957, Russell Prohl, author of *Woman in the Church*, commented: "There are a number of Bible critics who suggest that Priscilla wrote the Epistle to the Hebrews. Some day we may learn that this is true."

As you file into the jury box to hear the case for Priscilla, may that day be at hand.

PRAYER FOR THE NAMING OF A STAR

A nameless star on a drifting sea
Agleam on the tide, beams hope to me
Out of the silence of centuries past
- Out of time's wilderness - shines at last.

Let Truth look down on banners unfurled
On luminous ramparts of the world
A beacon wherever its radiance flows,
And a star be named where the true light glows.

- Ruth Hoppin

CHAPTER ONE

WE ARE WITNESSES TO A MYSTERY

A Profusion of Authors and Paul in Particular

In Apostolic times a remarkable letter was written to a group of Christians by one of their spiritual leaders. A few years later, copies were circulated to churches in other locations. The first century church was admonished by its zeal and discernment and uplifted by its stirring prose. This letter eventually found its way into the New Testament canon and is know to us as The Epistle to the Hebrews. In a tangled strand of history, deep mystery surrounds the name of the author.

A literary and theological masterpiece, the letter was much too good to be without an author - either real or pseudonymous. Before long the names of several leaders of the church became attached to it. Clement of Rome, Barnabas and Paul were the foremost candidates. Luke, Philip, Silas and others "also ran". Instead of solving the mystery, such expedients only multiplied confusion, for not one of these names was universally accepted. Time has obscured the truth with competing theories of authorship. Each theory is dogged by evidence that contradicts it - except one that I hope to demonstrate is true - or totally devoid of any evidence at all - and must be dismissed.

Hebrews is seldom ascribed to Paul nowadays, and belief in the Pauline authorship of Hebrews should not be considered a test of orthodoxy. If he didn't write it, what virtue can there be in thinking that he did?

There has not always been agreement that Paul either did or did not write Hebrews. In first century Alexandria a theory emerged that the letter to the Hebrews is a free translation of Paul's words, or a paraphrase of his thoughts.[1] Along the same line, in 1914 the Pontifical Biblical Commission stated:

> "Criteria of language and content prove that Paul was the author. Yet it is not necessary to assume that Paul gave the Epistle its form"[2]

One must be impressed by the persistence of this theory, but there is little to substantiate it. Imagine Paul employing a ghostwriter! Consider this unique document - its artistry, originality, and literary excellence. Despite affinities with Paul's thought, surely it is the product of the author's own mind.

Why might some people still think of Paul as the author of Hebrews? His name is part of the title of the letter in the King James Bible, and may be unquestioned for that reason alone. The author's conversion,[3] mediated by those who saw and heard Jesus, so at variance with the conversion of Paul, is overlooked. The apologetic tone of the postscript, to be discussed in detail later, and the absence of Paul's usual signature go unnoticed. This should not be so. Nor can we attribute the chasm between the style and vocabulary of Hebrews and the letters of Paul to differences in subject matter - and these criteria alone should disqualify him.

An Anonymous Letter?

Did the author in fact send an anonymous letter? After all, the identity of the author must have been known to the recipients. How else can we explain the request for prayer that the author be restored to them sooner?[4] Westcott, in his monumental work, declares the author did nothing to hide his identity.[5] This is perfectly true. Did the author merely fail to sign his name? Or was the name "lost" in some other way?

The crux of the matter is the omission of personal greetings, where the name of the author usually occurs, at the beginning of Hebrews. Some scholars conclude it is not a letter at all, but a study paper. This assumption runs into real trouble in the ending, where personal greetings are present. Nor does it follow where the message ineluctably leads - to a cluster of churches in a specific location where the author had a teaching ministry. He knew the recipients well enough to be dissatisfied with their progress. From the past, he recounts evidence of their faith.

With affection and chiding, he scores their present apathy. Hebrews is an epistle, and the author was known to the original recipients.

However, unlike other contemporaneous letters, the letter to the Hebrews has no prescript, with the author's name. Never was an opening sentence so conspicuous by its absence. Was it left out intentionally? If so, by whom - and why? Did someone decide to do away with the prescript? A motive would not be hard to find. By suppressing the name of the author, the letter could be assigned to Paul - much to the liking of certain elements in the church. Or did the author - or friends of the author omit the prescript when copies were circulated, in order to secure acceptance for the letter? In a completely different scenario, could the loss of the prescript be accidental?

The latter possibility is too remote to be taken seriously. This is the scholarly consensus.[6] The facts in the case are simple and clear. We have about 14,000 letters from the ancient world.[7] Many are originals. Not one lacks the usual greetings.[8] There is no record of the prescript alone becoming lost from any papyrus roll.[9] If Hebrews is an exception, it is the only exception we know of. Technically, the prescript is one sentence containing the name of the sender, the name of the recipient, and the preliminary greetings. (Paul customarily used two sentences.)[10] Since the introductory greeting is so brief, its loss would inevitably include part of the remainder of the writing.[11] It is more likely that the prescript was left out by the author. The sentence we know as Hebrews 1:1 is highly alliterative - and a perfectly good beginning. The "mystery of the missing prescript" deepens to "the mystery of the missing author."

Loss of the Author's Name

The loss of the author's name occurred very early, creating the world's most provocative "whodunit." Both riddle and clue: the exalted nature of the epistle, and by inference, the conspicuousness of the writer in the early church.

Although the author was known to the first recipients, we have seen that when copies were circulated from Rome, at a certain time, the name was omitted. The prominence of women in the church was falling out of favor, and the name was omitted either to suppress its female authorship, or to protect the letter itself from suppression. A telling circumstance is that Clement, Bishop of Rome, made extensive use of Hebrews in his Epistle to Corinthians, 95-96 A.D., but never said who he was quoting. By contrast, Clement did mention Paul when quoting *him.*

Harnack, citing Zahn, argued that since the letter was attributed at one time to Barnabas, and also to Paul, there must have been a time when it circulated anonymously. He reasoned that most likely, the identity of the author was suppressed intentionally.

Gilbert Bilezikian, a teacher of biblical studies at Wheaton College, remarks on "the conspiracy of anonymity...in the ancient church," and reasons:

> The lack of any firm data concerning the identity of the author in the extant writings of the church suggests a deliberate blackout more than a case of collective loss of memory.[12]

But why? The riddle is solved, of course, if Priscilla were the author.

Five years after Harnack's article was published, Friedrich Schiele forcefully supported his hypothesis. Writing in *The American Journal of Theology,* he countered the claim that the authorship of Hebrews could not be known. He then proceeded to defend the likelihood of Priscilla's authorship. Schiele declared that the anonymity of Hebrews was unique in the New Testament and related literature. In the case of letters, the author's name was of prime importance and easiest to preserve, but *should it be lost a pseudonym would customarily be provided.* He wrote:

> The anonymity of the Epistle to the Hebrews appears so peculiar and abnormal that it urgently demands an explanation...Why has just this epistle lost its author's name without the substitution of a better one?..*Harnack's Prisca hypothesis furnishes a complete and satisfying solution.*[13]

Schiele gave a second reason why we should not abandon the search for the author's identity: "the circle of Paul's friends is so well known that it would be surprising if from among its many names, that of the author...did not...appear." In other words, *we virtually have a list of names in which it appears.*

A more recent writer who noted the issue of "anonymity" is A. Victor Murray[14] who conceded that the epistle may have been written by Priscilla *"and this would account for the name of the author being omitted."* Yet, others have agonized over the loss of the author's name without giving a clue that Harnack and his supporters find a reasonable explanation in feminine authorship of the epistle. D. A. Hayes[15] realizes that the author was well known to the original recipients. So well known, in fact, that his style was immediately recognizable. It seemed unnecessary to "chronicle his name," Hayes explains, "so to-day he is...The Great Unknown." Hayes goes on to say that uncertainty over the author's name, going far back into antiquity, is "one of the strangest facts in all literature," and the chance that the author was not commemorated in scripture is simply incredible. Still no mention of Harnack or Priscilla.

Hayes remarked that Hebrews entered the New Testament canon on a cloud of mystery. How fortunate this document was not lost to us along with the author! What a sad commentary on human nature and sober warning to us that its authenticity was tied to the question: Did Paul write it? What a loss to the Christian world if its inclusion in the New Testament canon, touch and go for three hundred years, had been prevented by hero-worship and prejudice. The Western church was more at fault, omitting it from the Muratorian Canon of the late second century and depreciating its value.[16] About this time, the Eastern church, theorizing but never proving the letter was Paul's, accepted it anyway.[17] Finally, it was attributed to Paul and arranged with his letters.

In the third century Chester Beatty Papyrus II, Hebrews appears after Romans.[18] Proximity to the letters of Paul was beginning to overcome its troublesome anonymity. In the fourth century manuscripts Vaticanus and Sinaiticus, it appears before the Pastorals,[19] Paul becoming the author by implication. Also, apostolic origin was imputed to the letter. At Alexandria, optiminism triumphed over doubt in the year 367 A.D. when the Easter letter of Athanasius stated Paul wrote fourteen epistles including Hebrews.[20] Further authorization was given by councils at Hippo in 393 A.D. and Carthage in 397 and 419 A.D[21]. The letter to the Hebrews was "in"!

Acceptance of Hebrews into the canon of the New Testament has given the world a compelling mystery and piqued the curiousity of scholars. The long struggle to realize the spiritual equality conferred by God adds relevance and impetus to the question: "Did a *woman* write Holy Scripture?"

James Hope Moulton, New Testament scholar and Greek lexicographer, writing in 1909, referred to the "man - or woman" who wrote Hebrews.[22] Years later, in his Greek Testament lexicon, Priscilla is referred to primarily in terms of Harnack's carefully reasoned hypothesis.[23]

However, according to another expositor, the Epistle to the Hebrews is the product of a masculine mind.[24] This noteworthy assumption stands all alone. It is not preceded by a line of reasoning, nor is it followed by one word of explanation. In the absence of further elucidation, we can only say that his conclusion may be the product of a closed mind!

We shall discover in the course of our investigation that quite the contrary, Hebrews appears to be the product of a feminine mind.

NOTES TO CHAPTER I

1. Brooke Foss Westcott, *The Epistle to the Hebrews: The Greek Text with Notes and Essays* (1st edition 1889, 2nd ed., 1892) (Grand Rapids: Wm. B. Eerdman's Publishing Co., 1955), p. lxvlxvi. This edition is published by special arrangement with the Macmillan Co.
2. Alfred Wikenhauser, *New Testament Introduction* transl. Joseph Cunningham (New York: Herder and Herder, 1958), p. 454.
3. Heb. 2:3.
4. Heb. 13:18, 19.
5. Westcott, *op. cit.*, p. lxxv.
6. Westcott, p. xxx.
7. Wikenhauser, *op. cit.*, p. 346.
8. *Ibid.*, p. 349.
9. *Ibid.*, p. 459.
10. *Ibid.*, p. 348, 9.
11. *Ibid.*, p. 349.
12. Gilbert Bilezikian, *Beyond Sex Roles* (Grand Rapids: Baker Book House, 1985), p. 302.
13. Friedrich Michael Schiele, "Harnack's 'Probabilia' Concerning the Address and Author of the Epistle to the Hebrews," *The American Journal of Theology*, 1905 (290-306) p. 292-3.
14. A. Victor Murray, *How to Know Your Bible* Boston: The Beacon Press, 1952, p. 160.
15. D. A. Hayes, *The Epistle to the Hebrews*, Biblical Introduction Series, New York, Cincinnati: The Methodist Book Concern, p. 18-21.
16. H. T. Andrews, "Hebrews," *The Abingdon Bible Commentary* ed., Frederick Carl Eiselen, Edwin Lewis and David G. Downey (New York: Abingdon-Cokesbury Press, 1929), p. 1299.
17. *Ibid.*
18. Stephen S. Smalley, "Hebrews," *Exploring New Testament Backgrounds* (copyright by Christianity Today, n.d.), p. 49.
19. *Ibid.*
20. Westcott, *op. cit.*, p. lxxii.

21. *Ibid.*, p. 1xxiii.

22. Moulton, James Hope, "New Testament Greek in the Light of Modern Discovery," *Essays on Some Biblical Questions of the Day*. London: Macmillan and Co., Limited, 1909.

23. Moulton, James Hope and Milligan, George, *The Vocabulary of the Greek Testament Illustrated from the papyri and other nonliterary sources*. London: Hodder and Stoughton, Limited, 1930.

24. Marcus Dods, "The Epistle to the Hebrews," *The Expositor's Greek Testament,* Vol. IV, ed. W. Robertson Nicoll (London and New York: Hodder & Stoughton, Limited), p. 229.

CHAPTER TWO

WE EXAMINE THE EVIDENCE

Can we ever know with reasonable certainty who wrote the Epistle to the Hebrews? What do we have to go on?

A tape-recorded interview with the author would be anachronistic but nice. We might settle for the original document, under glass in a museum, even if it were slightly frayed around the edges and still without a signature. Lacking this kind of evidence we must look to the Bible and certain elucidative non-Biblical sources. In the New Testament, Acts and Hebrews will be our primary guide, with mention of First Corinthians, Romans, II Timothy and the Revelation of John. Old Testament references are exceptionally numerous in Hebrews. These include the sixth chapter of Zechariah and several psalms. Apocryphal writings (N.T.), ancient manuscripts, and the Dead Sea Scrolls will be placed in evidence. The Roman catacombs are to reveal key secrets.

Step by step, our study will lead us to the author of Hebrews.

The Original Title and How it Grew

The Epistle to the Hebrews has nearly as many "titles" as "authors." Look at the list and take your choice:

TRANSLATION	TITLE
King James Version	The Epistle of Paul the Apostle to the Hebrews
Revised Standard Version and New Revised Standard Version	The Letter to the Hebrews
Jerusalem Bible	The Letter to the Hebrews
New English Bible	A Letter to Hebrews
Revised English Bible	A Letter to Hebrews
The Authentic New Testament (transl. Schonfield)	Anonymous Homily to the Hebrews
Novum Testamentum Graece Hebrews (transl. Souter)	The Epistle of Paul to the Hebrews
The Holy Bible (Catholic) (transl. Ronald Knox)	The Epistle of the Blessed Apostle Paul to the Hebrews
The New American Bible (Catholic)	The Epistle to the Hebrews
Expositor's Greek New Testament	The Epistle of Paul the Apostle to the Hebrews (with note that it should be: To the Hebrews)

The King James Version has the word "apostle", but Souter does not use it. This is a discrepancy even though both titles have the name of Paul. Further embellishment occurs in Knox's translation with the word "Blessed." Despite these ascriptions, Paul's name was not part of the original title.

The oldest manuscripts have the title "pros hebraios" (to the Hebrews).[1] Codex Claromontanus (Manuscript "D") has no title, but a running heading "to Hebrews."[2] Two Egyptian versions of good authenticity and antiquity have "to the Hebrews."[3] In the evolution of the title, first the word "Epistle" was added. Paul's name came in later.[4] Which one is right? The title: "To the Hebrews" is very early, if not original.

Papyrus and Parchment

Now we should inquire if material editorial alterations have crept into the text of Hebrews. We have at least 4500 Greek manuscripts. Some are only small fragments of papyrus, but fifty or so contain the entire New Testament.[5] In the case of Hebrews, variations in the text are relatively minor and do not pertain to our discussion in any significant way. On the evidence of the best manuscripts, there is no reason to believe that any important part was added or deleted.

The original text of New Testament writings was likely written on papyrus.[6] Papyrus was not very durable, but the early Christians could not easily afford parchment. Paul asked for certain parchment leaves "above all" in II Timothy 4:13. These may have been Old Testament books. In better times the New Testament would be copied on parchment, by decree of Constantine but not before the fourth century.[7]

The rough surface of papyrus made cursive writing difficult. This is why the earliest manuscripts have "uncial" or "majuscule" writing. "Uncial" is Latin for "inch". The letters - all capitals - were an inch high.

So, the parchments with majuscule writing are the oldest. Of these, Codex Vaticanus ("B"), from the middle of the fourth century, is the earliest we have.[8] It is complete through Heb. 9:14a, but lacks Heb. 14b to the end of the New Testament. Only Codex Sinaiticus (א) has all the New Testament (including Hebrews) in uncial letters.[9] Written in the fourth century, this is perhaps the best manuscript.[10]

Other reliable manuscripts containing the whole text of Hebrews are:[11]

* Codex Alexandrinus ("A") - from the first half of the fifth century.
* Codex Claramontanus ("D") - a collection of the epistles of Paul from the sixth century.
* Codex Ephraemi - a fifth century palimpsest.

* Codex Porphyrianus - a ninth century palimpsest.
* Codex Athous Laurae (ψ) - from the eighth or ninth century (complete except for Heb. 8:11-9:19).

In addition, we have an Egyptian version - the Memphitic which represents a Greek text of "great excellence."[12]

Of course, many copies of Hebrews were made on papyrus. Most of these have disintegrated, leaving pieces of the text, and hinting at the fate of the original letter. An example of papyrus fragmentation is "P13", from about 300 A.D., with Heb. 2:14-5:5 and parts of chapters 10, 11 and 12.[13] However, there is a papyrus codex, discovered in Egypt, with the complete text of Hebrews. This important document, known as Chester Beatty Papyrus II or P46, is a collection of Paul's letters, except for the Pastorals. As we have seen, in P46 Hebrews was placed immediately after Romans, telling us that Hebrews was considered one of Paul's letters. (By contrast, in the Latin West, Paul was NOT considered the author.)

If we were to look for the autograph, or original manuscript of Hebrews, the closest we come in time is P46, written in the third century,[14] and perhaps as early as 200 A.D.[15] We cannot follow the letter any further into antiquity.

Still, we can try to understand the mind of the author as disclosed in the letter. Empathy will help us as we turn our attention to his (or her) use of personal pronouns.

Pronouns: Plural and Singular

We needn't comment on the use of the plural pronoun "we" or "us" in a letter, when it obviously refers to the writer and readers collectively. But when used as a first person reference, "we" hints at one or more close associates. Its careful construction and distinctive style argue against joint authorship of Hebrews. This by no means precludes the possibility of two or more persons talking over the subject matter. As we know, Hebrews alternates doctrinal reasoning and exhortation. The chart below will show that first person references are singular in presenting the main argument, and equally divided between plural and singular in digressions to spur the faith of the readers.

FIRST-PERSON REFERENCES[16]

Singular ("I" or "Me")		***Plural ("We" or "Us")***	
Doctrine	*Exhortation*	*Doctrine*	*Exhortation*
			Heb. 6:9 "Though *we* speak thus, yet in your case, beloved, *we* feel sure of better things that belong to salvation."
			Heb. 6:11 "And *we* desire each one of you to show the same earnestness..."
Heb. 11:32 "And what shall *I* say? For time would fail *me* to tell..."			
			Heb. 13:18 "Pray for *us*, for *we* are sure that we have a clear conscience..."
	Heb. 13:19 "I urge you the more earnestly do this in order that *I* may be restored to you the sooner."		
	Heb. 13:22 "*I* appeal to you, brethren, bear with *my* word of exhortation, for *I* have written to you briefly."		
	Heb. 13.23 "... *I* shall see you ..."		

The pronoun "we" in Heb. 6:9 and 11 and the alternation of "we" in Heb. 13:18 and "I" in Heb. 13:19,22 and 23 is a sign the author is speaking in behalf of an ally whom the readers know. In particular, the plea "Pray for us" (Heb. 13:18) denotes the author plus one other person or a small group of specific persons. Although Paul used "we," meaning himself and other apostles, it cannot mean a general category - such as religious leaders - in Heb. 13:18, for the reader is to pray for their return. How can the plural pronoun be explained?

The question is answered in a simple, logical way if we hypothesize that "we" means Priscilla and Aquila, a married couple who were inseparable. Their names are mentioned six times in the New Testament - never one without the other. Priscilla (or Aquila) used the singular "I" in presenting the main argument, changing to the plural "we" in exhorting the readers. They both cared very much for the spiritual standing of the readers. After all, they were at one time or another co-leaders of churches in Rome, Corinth and Ephesus.

We Find Clues in the Postscript

For the investigator in search of evidence to support Harnack's theory, the postscript (Heb. 13:22-25) is a treasure trove. Here is the allusion to Timothy, a coworker, linking the author to Paul. Harnack deduced that the author or authors were at least on the same level with Timothy as church leaders, and being of Paul's most intimate circle, are named in scripture.

In fact, verses 23 and 24 contain no fewer than six clues concerning the identity of the author, and the destination and place of origin of the letter. Briefly stated, they are:

(1) The author is closely associated with Timothy.

(2) Timothy and the author are away from the locale of their ministry and plan to return as soon as they can.

(3) Timothy is in a place where his freedom has been limited by custody or imprisonment.

(4) The author, in the same general location as Timothy, or near by, is free to travel.

(5) The recipients have several leaders in addition to the author and Timothy (see also Heb. 13:17).

(6) "They of Italy" send greetings.

These clues will yield material evidence for the destination of the letter, its place of origin, and the identity of the writer. However, they do not exhaust the rich mine of information to be found in this portion of the epistle. Let's focus our attention on Heb. 13:22.

Hebrews 13:22

Strangely apologetic is the first sentence in the postscript: "I appeal to you, brethren, bear with my word of exhortation, for I have written to you briefly."

What impelled a brilliant, articulate leader like the author of Hebrews to justify the writing of his message? Exactly what did he mean? By calling attention to its brevity, he could have meant:

(1) "Be patient with my word of exhortation and read it, since the message is short." Or

(2) "Forgive me for writing too briefly. By compressing the message, I have not done justice to the theme."

In either case his plea merits our attention.

Actually, Hebrews is not very brief, as New Testament letters go. In the Greek language, the thirteen epistles of Paul average about 1300 words.[17] In the English language, they average 3,300 words:

Epistle	Approximate number of words (KJV)[18]
Romans	9,400
I Corinthians	9,500
II Corinthians	6,100
Galatians	3,100
Ephesians	3,000
Philippians	2,000
Colossians	2,000
I Thessalonians	1,900
II Thessalonians	1,000
I Timothy	2,300
II Timothy	1,700
Titus	900
Philemon	450
Average:	3,335
Hebrews:	6,900

Hebrews has about 6,900 words. It is longer than eleven of Paul's thirteen epistles, and more than twice as long as the average. (Paul's authorship of Ephesians is in dispute.) Hebrews can be compared with Romans, in being a dissertation on a theme. Romans is not much longer.

New Testament epistles are usually longer than business and social letters of the ancient world. Extant letters on papyrus range from 18 to 209 words, averaging 87.[19] The letters of Cicero do not exceed 2,530 words, averaging 295; and those of Seneca do not exceed 4,134 words, averaging 995.[20] What reason had the author of Hebrews, well versed in literature and philosophy, to call his message "brief"? Certainly, his remark: "I have written to you briefly" raises a question. *Hebrews is not a short letter*. Therefore, did the author imply that he failed to do justice to the subject by treating it with undue brevity? It seems to me he covered all the ground thoroughly. The basic theme can be stated adequately in much less space. Well then, what did he mean?

To understand Hebrews 13:22 we must consider the Greek word ἐπιστέλλο "to send a message in writing" and the alternative meaning "to enjoin or command." To say the author "wrote briefly" is a proper translation, but we have seen that it does create a problem. Linguistically, the meaning "to enjoin or command" is equally defensible. As for the word βραχύs translated "briefly" - it also means "little" indicating degree or time. Schonfield picks this up in his translation:

> I beg you, brother, bear with this message of exhortation, for indeed *only to a slight extent have I given you orders*[21] (italics mine).

Now, compare I Peter 5:12:

> By Silvanus, a faithful brother as I regard him, I have *written briefly* to you, exhorting and declaring that this is the true grace of God; stand fast in it (italics mine).

Again we have the translation "written briefly," but this time both Greek words are different. γράφω is used instead ἐπιστέλλω. No meaning other than "write" can be derived from γράφω. Instead of βραχύs the word translated "briefly" is ὀλίγων meaning "in a few words." In order to convey "to a slight degree" the expression πρὸs ὀλίγον would have been used. From the context of Peter's statement we can easily see that no apology was implied. Schonfield's translation, "only to a slight extent have I given you orders," is entirely justified by the Greek text.

Schonfield was not the only scholar to prefer this translation. L. Paul Trudinger pointed out that while the epistle is not brief, the words of instruction and command are brief. Thus, the author could logically plead for patience with the few words in which the readers were "enjoined" or "instructed." Trudinger notes that ἐπιστέλλω often carries this meaning in classical Greek, and cites the noted authorities J. H. Moulton and G. Milligan who support this view. This is his translation of Heb. 13:22:

> I appeal to you, brothers, bear with my words of instruction and admonition, *for my commands have been but brief* (italics mine)[22]

In view of its highly meritorious prose and spiritual authoritativeness, we are compelled to ask: who would end the treatise with an outright apology? Who would apologize for having given orders - only a little?

Was the author a *woman*?[23]

In our search for the author, evidence found in the closing chapter of Hebrews is significant. To us it is clear the thirteenth chapter was written by the author, referring as it does to his preceding remarks. Stylistic considerations verify the unity of the epistle, despite the relative informality of the conclusion. Verse 22 explicitly relates the writer of the postscript to the rest of the letter. Nonetheless, the authenticity of the thirteenth chapter has been questioned. Similarly, the suggestion has been made that someone else wrote verses 23, 24 and 25. But compare verse 23 with verse 19, which is not in the postscript. The hope of returning soon is expressed in both.

R. V. G. Masker, writing in *The Expository Times*, argued in defense of "The Integrity of the Epistle to the Hebrews," making the point that there is no manuscript evidence to the contrary:

> ... so far as we know, Hebrews was never in circulation without the closing chapter. In no Greek MSS and in no extant version is there evidence to the contrary. Clement of Rome as early as 96 uses the language of ch. 13, and ... the *prima facie* assumption is that he knew the Epistle as we now have it .... In the central portion of He 13 the writer returns to some of the main thoughts of the letter,...[24]

Tasker is right that based on internal evidence, and lack of manuscript evidence to the contrary, the integrity of the epistle must be maintained. Another commentator, William Lane, comments on "the very evident links" between chapter 13 and the preceding material. Vocabulary, style, structure, and the use of quotations from the Pentateuch and the Psalms, all signify a single author:

> ...chap. 13 transmits an essential message that can scarcely be separated from the concerns and conceptual themes expressed in Heb 1-12.[25]

The thirteenth chapter, with its tantalizing postscript naming Timothy, will aid our search for the author. The groundless assertion that Paul wrote verses 23-25 is perhaps a panicky conclusion, because it is no secret that Timothy was a leader of the church in Ephesus for years. So were Priscilla and Aquila.

Take another look at Heb. 13:22. What leader of the early church composed this remarkable document and ended it with an implicit apology? A more comprehensive question is: what can we learn about the personality of the author from the letter? As we examine the evidence, our next task is to construct a psychological profile.

NOTES TO CHAPTER II

1. Smalley, *op. cit.*, p. 49 and Westcott, *op. cit.*, p. xxvii.
2. Westcott, p. xxvii.
3. *Ibid.*
4. *Ibid.*
5. Wikenhauser, *op. cit.*, p. 78.
6. *Ibid.*, p. 67.
7. *Ibid.*, p. 65.
8. *Ibid.*, p. 79.
9. T. Robertson, "The Transmission of the New Testament," *The Abingdon Bible Commentary*, ed. Frederick Carl Eiselen *et al.* (New York: Abingdon-Cokesbury Press, 1929), p. 862.
10. G. S. Wegener, *6000 Years of the Bible* (New York: Harper & Row, 1963), p. 286.
11. Westcott, p. xv.
12. Westcott, p. xx.
13. Wikenhauser, p. 87.
14. *Ibid.*
15. Philip W. Comfort, *Early Manuscripts and Modern Translations of the New Testament* (Wheaton: Tyndale House Publishers, 1990), p. 51.
16. NOTE: In Heb. 8:1, the Greek text does not favor either the singular pronoun, as in the New English Bible, or the plural pronoun, as in the Revised Standard Version and King James Bible. Heb. 8:1 may be translated: "The main point of what has been said..." rather than "Now this is *my* main point" (NEB) or "Now the point in what *we* are saying is this:..." (RSV). All italics are mine.
17. Wikenhauser, p. 347.
18. The Holy Bible, authorized King James version, *New Encyclopedic Reference Edition* (Grand Rapids: Zondervan Publishing House, 1996, copyright by Royal Publishers, Inc., Nashville, Tenn.).
19. Wikenhauser, p. 346.
20. *Ibid.*

21. Hugh J. Schonfield, ed. and transl., *The Authentic New Testament* (New York: The New American Library of World Literature, Inc., 1958), p. 364.

22. L. Paul Trudinger, "A Note on Heb. 13:22," *Journal of Theological Studies* 23 (1972) 128-130, citing J. H. Moulton and G. Milligan, *The Vocabulary of the Greek New Testament* (Grand Rapids, 1952), pp. 245-6.

23. We are reminded of the *The Epistle of Maria the Proselyte to Ignatius*, in which she concludes with a disclaimer that she does not write to instruct him. Cynthia Briggs Kittredge, "Hebrews," *Searching the Scriptures*, Vol. 2. (NY: Crossroad, 1993-94), p. 433, citing *Ante-Nicene Fathers* I, p. 120-123.

24. R. V. G. Tasker, "The Integrity of the Epistle to the Hebrews," *Expository Times* 47 (1935-36) 136-38.

25. William L. Lane, *Word Biblical Commentary, Volume 47A, Hebrews 1-8* (Dallas: Word Books, Publisher, 1991), Introduction, p. lxviii.

CHAPTER THREE

WE CONSTRUCT A PSYCHOLOGICAL PROFILE: IS THE AUTHOR FEMININE?

In our search for the author of Hebrews, we have not unearthed a sealed envelope with the name inside but we do have a letter and the ability to reason about it. If you were to send a letter to churches in your home city expressing your deepest religious concerns, think how much you would reveal about yourself - by what you choose to say or leave unsaid, the scripture you quote, your style and vocabulary. If you stressed the importance of faith in family life, and instruction to children; if you mentioned women as well as men whose lives have been an inspiration to you - then your readers might tend to assume that YOU were a woman, even if your letter were unsigned.

In reading through the Epistle to the Hebrews in order to delineate the author, we shall ask two distinct but related questions: Is the author *feminine*? And does the author *identify with women*?

First, is the author *feminine?* That is, in careful perusal of the letter do we discern a feminine, rather than a masculine mind? In asking this question, I do not imply that the main development of thought can be attributed to one sex or the other. Rather, we are to seek clues in the personality, mode of expression, and status of the writer.

Of all New Testament literature outside the gospels, the letter to the Hebrews is most *illustrative of the humanity and compassion of Christ.* Two examples:

> Therefore he had to become like has brothers and sisters in every respect, so that he might be a merciful and faithful high priest in the service of God, to make a sacrifice of atonement for the sins of the people. Because he himself was tested by what he had suffered, he is able to help those who are being tested.
>
> (Heb. 2:17-18 NRSV)

> For we do not have a high priest who is unable to sympathize with our weaknesses, but we have one who in every respect has been tested as we are, yet without sin.
>
> (Heb. 4:15 NRSV)

With empathy for priest and people, the author expresses the essential characteristic of every high priest: *"He is able to deal gently with the ignorant and wayward, since he himself is subject to weakness"* (Heb. 5:2 NRSV).

Alongside a keen depiction of the compassion *of* Christ, we find in Hebrews compassion *for* Christ. In all verses cited above the vulnerability of Christ to suffering, and his experience of suffering, are portrayed. Throughout his lifetime, Jesus prayed and beseeched God "with loud cries and tears" (Heb. 5:7), according to the author, who perceived that his mission, by its very nature, entailed suffering (Heb. 5:8,9).

In the twelfth chapter, we find a reference to both the physical and psychological suffering endured for our salvation. The shame of the cross and the hostility of sinners are alluded to (v. 2,3), showing a perceptiveness for the emotional aspect of Jesus' ordeal. In the thirteenth chapter, we are admonished to "go to Jesus outside the camp," in the sense of being willing to bear abuse, as he did (v. 12, 13).

The motif of suffering along with those in physical or psychological pain is characteristic of the author. Our psychological portrait is beginning to reveal an unusually sympathetic individual, who is able and willing to share the emotions of other people, and regards them with a certain tenderness.

This person admonishes others to evince the same trait. In the tenth chapter, the readers are encouraged to remember their own trials. There is an interesting reference in v. 33 to being partners with those who were mistreated. This situation was akin to being mistreated oneself.

Compassion for those who were in prison is recalled and commended (v. 34). In the words of the author:

> Remember those who are in prison, as though you were in prison with them; those who are being tortured, as though you yourselves were being tortured.
>
> (Heb. 13:3, NRSV).

An interesting example of the sympathetic nature of the author is found in Heb. 11:21, where the aged patriarch Jacob is described as leaning on his staff when blessing the sons of Joseph. A. Nairne cites "leaning on his staff" as an "otiose addition," "a pathetic detail," in fact, an example of the author's "imagination of sympathy."[1]

Our psychological portrait must depict empathy as well as sympathy. Our author understood the feelings and the reasoning of Moses' parents when they hid him for three months after his birth, in order to save his life. The reasons for this act of faith were: his parents saw that Moses was a beautiful child, and they were not afraid to defy the king's edit.

Now we should consider a most revealing statement: when Moses was grown *he refused to be called a son of Pharaoh's daughter* (Heb. 11:24). The author understood that Pharaoh's daughter looked upon Moses as a son. James Alexander Robertson, a scholar who supported Harnack's Priscilla theory, had this to say about the allusions to Moses:

> The tenderness of the reason given for the hiding of the infant Moses by his parents is striking - "because they saw he was a beautiful child." So also is the description of Moses' act of faith - "he refused to be called the son of Pharaoh's daughter."[2]

Yes, by faith, Moses repudiated the Egyptian court in order to cast his lot with the Israelite people. Here is something to ponder: *his momentous decision was worded in terms of his relationship with his "foster mother."*

These points should be made in connection with the allusions to Moses in the eleventh chapter of Hebrews. First, the act of his mother (both parents, in the Greek Septuagint, known to the author) narrated in Genesis, ch. 2 was elevated to an exemplary act of faith. Second, a woman, more likely than a man, would think of the riven relationship between Moses and Pharaoh's daughter.

Next, let us turn our attention to the author's selection of other Old Testament scripture. We have already discerned a poignant portrayal of Christ, and, as Josephine Massyngberde Ford put it, "glimpses of Jesus' character...which would be especially appealing to a woman - compassion, gentleness, and understanding of human weakness." She goes on to say that:

> No New Testament writing exhibits such a unique and delicate poise between the human and divine nature of Jesus ... so clearly as does the Epistle to the Hebrews.[3]

One revealing example of scripture selection is found in Heb 8:9, recalling Jer. 31:32. God is here shown as taking the people of Israel by the hand to lead them out of Egypt. George Wesley Buchanan, in his commentary, writes:

> The picture of a father holding his small son's hand to keep him from getting lost or hurt is painted of the Lord...[4]

A second example is the reference to Melchizedek in the seventh chapter. First the author gives a "mini-lesson", analyzing the literal meaning of "Melchizedek, king of

Salem." We are told the appellation means "King of righteousness, king of peace." This instructional aside hints at the author's interest in education. In verse three, we are told that Melchizedek is "without father or mother" - not an uncommon way of referring to supernatural beings, in classical times. However, as J. A. Robertson noted, "a certain pathos" may be perceived. What indeed was in the mind of the author of Hebrews, in describing Melchizedek as an orphan? Was it merely a matter of convention, or was it a flash of compassionate insight?

Robertson, in common with other scholars, finds that "The writer is deeply interested in facts concerning parenthood and childhood",[5] and cites examples.

Before we look at some of these examples, you may wish to read through the epistle and trace references to childhood, education, and parental discipline.

Have you paused at Heb. 5:11-14, a passage which chides the readers for being immature and stresses education of the moral faculties? Did you note the passage in chapter twelve on parental discipline: "God is treating you as children; for what child is there whom a parent does not discipline?... Moreover, we had human parents to discipline us, and we respected them..." (Heb. 12:7-11).

The author has even more to say on the topic of parental discipline, having thought deeply on the subject. We are told that human parents, unlike God, are fallible in their judgment: "they disciplined us...as seemed best to them,"... v. 10. "As seemed best to them" - by implication, they do not always achieve the favorable results they desire for their children. Furthermore, their training is "for a short time," ending when adulthood is reached.[6]

In constructing our psychological profile, consider that the tone of these admonitions is feminine. That is to say - do they sound like Paul, or Apollos, or Barnabas? Or do they sound more like - your mother, perhaps?

To sum up so far: the author's concern with education is a prominent characteristic - ranging from the moral education of children to instruction in the tenets of faith for all believers .

Empathetic and sympathetic, the writer is tuned into the physical and mental suffering of Christ, and those who suffer for their faith.

To continue with our psychological profile: various commentators on the author's style note a striking delicacy of expression. Nairne remarks on the epistle's "classical purity," the "distinguished character of the vocabulary," "fastidiousness" in the choice of words. Subtlety of expression is surely the outward sign of a subtle thinker. Is delicacy of expression not the sign of a refined, elegant personality? We would not have to go far afield to characterize this writer as cultured, perfectionist, and dainty.

A modern commentator states: "The best Greek composition in the New Testament is in this letter, and so delicate and persuasive is it that there are those who think they detect a woman's hand" - and consider that Priscilla, as Paul's close friend, may have been the writer.[7]

A strong advocate for Harnack's theory was Mildred A. R. Tuker, whose article, "The Gospel According to Prisca" was published in 1913.[8] She finds a sharp contrast in the writings of Paul and the epistle, despite the many similarities in theology and areas of discussion. In Heb. 13:4, Tuker finds a dignified allusion to personal morality, stated in equalitarian terms. There is no differentiation according to sex, no overstatement, nothing explicit.

Paul's acceptance of Priscilla and other women as coworkers in proclaiming the faith has been blurred by certain comments "designed to subordinate the one sex to the other," as Tuker states it.

She notes the absence of any such comments in Hebrews.

She then pauses at Heb. 13:18,19 to notice an oddity: the author exhorts "pray for us... I beseech you all the more to do this that I may be restored to you the sooner" (or "very soon"). By the way, the words translated "I beseech you more abundantly" in Heb. 13:19 can be translated idiomatically as "with all my heart I ask you" or "with all the strength I have I plead with you."[9]

Now, this may be subjective, according to Tuker, but it strikes her that the change from plural to singular in this case, and the phraseology "I urge you to pray all the more that I may return to you sooner" is less typical of a male than a female writer:

> "...it is not natural that Aquila should write: 'Pray for us...I exhort you the more to do this that I may be restored to you the sooner.' It is natural and affectionate in Priscilla."

Before we leave these intriguing verses, take another look at them: "Pray for *us*: (for *we* trust *we* have a good conscience...) *I* beseech you all the more abundantly (to pray) in order that *I* may be restored to you the sooner."

The change from plural to singular is provocative, because prayer for more than one person is requested; indicating that more than one person is away from the readers. Why, then, the singular "that *I* may be restored to you"? The singular "*I* beseech" is understandable, for a single author is writing but why "Pray for *us*...that *I* may be restored..."?

A reasonable explanation is that the author represented a married couple. Because of theological affinities of the epistle with Paul's letters, and instances of similar phraseology, (and the reference to Timothy) we must look for the author in the circle of Paul's closest associates. In addition, as these verses suggest - and as Harnack suggested we should be looking for a married couple close to Paul.

Let's take a parting look at the same two verses, this time with attention to the slightly apologetic tone of v. 18: "we are sure that we have a clear conscience, desiring to act honorably in all things." A modern scholar, Gilbert Bilezikian, sets this verse alongside the appeal in Heb. 13:22: "I appeal to you, brethren, bear with my word of exhortation, for I have written to you briefly" (or, "only to a slight extent have I given you orders.")

He remarks that Priscillan authorship would explain "a number of semi-apologetic pleas for credibility found in the Epistle," including the two examples cited above. Bilezikian goes on to say that such statements "seem to address a hindrance that pertains to the status of the author without constituting a reason for disqualification as a doctor of the church."

Bilezikian continues:

> The (Priscilla) theory would also account for the baffling remark made by the author prior to delving into high doctrine, "This we will do if God permits" (6:33). Rather than expressing confidence that death will not strike with the next dip of the pen, this statement seems to appeal to divine authority in pressing on to the exposition of the deeper dimensions of the Christian faith.
>
> Likewise, the mention of the author's travel plans as a companion of Timothy would make sense for a woman teacher desirous of receiving from Paul's male disciple the guarantee of his advocacy...
>
> Such references would constitute subtle hints of the author's understanding of the limitations pertaining to her status in a code language comprehensible to those readers aware of her identity.[10]

Bilezikian also notes a tone of deference toward the readers' spiritual leaders, even intimating that the letter was written under their auspices. This, he claims, would explain the curious nature of the document, which is at once a letter and a treatise. A fifth century writer, Theodoret, had an interesting comment on Heb. 13:17, which exhorts the reader:

> "Obey your leaders and submit to them, for they are keeping watch over your souls and will give an account. Let them do this with joy..."

Theodoret said:

> This way of speaking intimates, that their rulers did not need such instruction; for which reason (the author) did not write to them, but to their disciples[11]

Another writer, Daniel Whitby, around the year 1700, made a similar observation:

> Hence it seems evident that this epistle was not sent to the bishops or rulers of the Church, but to the whole Church, or the laity...[12]

All these considerations lend credence to the observation that the author was somehow under constraint despite having an obvious leadership role.

Focusing again on Heb. 13:17: "Let them (your leaders) do this with joy and not with sighing - for that would be harmful to you." (NRSV). Does it seem to you that a woman, more likely than a man, would express concern for the happiness of church leaders? That concern extends to the flock: if leaders are unhappy, their people will suffer as a result.

Gentle tact and diplomacy are a hallmark of the epistle. From the very first sentence, the validity of God's past revelation is assumed: God spoke to the readers' ancestors and through the prophets; today that revelation is carried further, through a Son (Heb. 1:1). When heroes of faith are enumerated in the eleventh chapter, sensitivity is shown to the readers' past. According to Peake:

> ...just as in earlier parts of the Epistle, so here his tactics are of a very conciliatory kind. He seeks for a point of contact with his readers, and tries to make them feel that what is most precious to them really supports the position to which he desires to bring them. 'I sympathise,' he would say, 'with all your enthusiasm for the great heroes...but you will best follow their example, not by falling back to the religious stage which they occupied, but by loyal adherence to Jesus, the supreme Person of history.[13]

"Is the author *feminine*?" To our first question, we have amassed ample evidence for feminine style and outlook. In our second question, "Does the author *identify with women*?" we wish to inquire if women of faith and their role in religious history are acknowledged - and by implication, their equality before God. This issue was relevant in apostolic times, and no less relevant today. An affirmative answer to *both* questions would constitute compelling evidence for a female author.

NOTES TO CHAPTER III

1. Alexander Nairne, *The Epistle to the Hebrews* (Cambridge: Cambridge University Press, 1957), p. cliv.

2. James Alex Robertson, *The Hidden Romance of the New Testament* (Boston: The Pilgrim Press; London: James Clarke & Co., Ltd. 1923), p. 179.

3. J. Massyngberde Ford, "The Mother of Jesus and The Authorship of the Epistle to the Hebrews," *The Bible Today* 82 (1976) p. 684 (Collegeville, MN: St. John's Abbey).

4. George Wesley Buchanan, *The Anchor Bible: To the Hebrews* (N.Y.: Doubleday, 1972) p. 138

5. Robertson, *op. cit.,* p. 179.

6. Kenneth S. Wuest, *Wuest's Word Studies: Hebrews in the Greek New Testament* (Grand Rapids: Eerdmans Publishing Company, 1947), p. 219-220.

7. Bruce Barton, *The Book Nobody Knows* (Cutchogue, N.Y.: Buccaneer Books, 1992), p. 99.

8. Mildred A.R. Tuker, "The Gospel According to Prisca," *Nineteenth Century* 73(1913)81-98.

9. Paul Ellingworth and Eugene A. Nida, *A Translator's Handbook on the Epistle to the Hebrews* (London, NY, Stuttgart: United Bible Societies, 1983), p. 333-4.

10. Gilbert Bilezikian, *op. cit.,* p. 302-3.

11. Adam Clarke, *Introduction to The Epistle of Paul the Apostle to the Hebrews*, p. 670.

12. *Ibid.*

13. Arthur S. Peake, *The Heroes and Martyrs of Faith (Studies in the Eleventh Chapter of the Epistle to the Hebrews)* (London: Hodder and Stoughton, 1910), p. 18,19.

CHAPTER FOUR

WE CONSTRUCT A PSYCHOLOGICAL PROFILE: DOES THE AUTHOR IDENTIFY WITH WOMEN?

A question arises naturally, logically, and inevitably from study of the eleventh chapter of Hebrews: "Does the author identify with women?" To a remarkable degree, the author acknowledges and values the example of leading women in the religious history of their people. Indeed, the eleventh, or so-called "Heroes of Faith" chapter is better named "Heroes and Heroines of Faith."

A cursory look at the eleventh chapter will reveal that two women, Sarah and Rahab, are mentioned by name among the faithful. Then, there is a curious reference to "women who received their dead by resurrection." At the end of the chapter the author states that despite the merit of all the faithful ones their faith - along with ours - was yet to be perfected in Jesus. Thus, the women who received their dead by resurrection were not women of New Testament times but of the Old Testament. *They cannot be mentioned by name because their names are not recorded in scripture*. Nonetheless, two specific women are alluded to: the widow of Zarephath whose son was restored to life by Elijah (I Kings 17:8-24) and the Shunammite woman whose son was resurrected by Elisha (2 Kings 4:18-37).

The author of Hebrews recounts the faith of these two women - faith which enabled these miraculous events to take place. If a man were telling the story, it would be reasonable to expect that the story would be told in a different way, with Elijah and Elisha the protagonists who did miraculous deeds by faith.

As a matter of fact, a man *did* tell the story. His name was Sirach and his story is in the apocryphal book Sirach, or Ecclesiasticus. And this is the way he told it:

> "How glorious you were, Elijah, in your wondrous deeds!...You raised a corpse from death and from Hades, by the word of the Most High..."
>
> (Sirach 48:4,5)

As for Elisha, we are told by Sirach:

> "Elisha...performed...marvels with every utterance of his mouth...Nothing was too hard for him, and when he was dead his body prophesied."
>
> (Sirach 48:12-13)

This is a far cry from women, through faith, receiving their dead by resurrection. Don't look for women at all in Sirach's roll call of heroes of faith. He begins with these words: "Let us now praise famous men" (Eccl. 44:1 Rev. Eng. Bible) and he means just that.

The author of Hebrews was familiar with the roll call of Heroes of Faith in Ecclesiasticus, for it was part of the Greek Septuagint. In fact, Hebrews follows right along with Ecclesiasticus, with mention of Enoch, Noah, Abraham, and Moses. But while Sirach mentions Abraham he does not name Sarah and while he extols Joshua he does not name Rahab. By contrast, the author of Hebrews alludes to Joshua but does not name him, but names Rahab instead, for her role in helping Joshua's spies. There is a reference to Rahab in James 2:25 in which she is described as "justified by works" in saving the spies, but in Hebrews there is a different "spin":

> "*By faith* Rahab the prostitute did not perish with those who were disobedient, because she had received the spies in peace."

Clement of Rome states twice that Rahab acted through faith (I Clem 12). He adds a new element of Rahab's spiritual discernment: "...not only faith, but prophecy, is found in the woman."[1]

The Massoretic (Hebrew) text of Joshua 2:1, - and the Greek Septuagint, used by the author - both describe Rahab as a prostitute. It can be argued and it *has* been argued that the inclusion of Rahab, a harlot, as a hero of faith is a bit far-fetched. But there she is in the eleventh chapter and the author of Hebrews placed her there.

It might be illuminating, however, to pay closer attention to Rahab, and how she was perceived in antiquity. Josephus, the first century Jewish historian, and some Rabbinic writers, did not regard Rahab as a prostitute, but as an innkeeper.

Josephus reports that Rahab knew about the imminent Israelite victory through signs from God. Prof. A. T. Hanson suggests that Josephus, by presenting Rahab as a prophetess, was a bridge between the New Testament and I Clement.[2]

Rahab may or may not have been a prostitute. We are reminded of Mary Magdalene, who "became" a prostitute in the fourth century, and was never regarded as such by the early church. In fact, several manuscripts have "Rahab, the *so-called* prostitute"[3] (italics mine).

Rahab may in fact have been a respectable innkeeper. G. Verkuyl, writing in *The Bible Translator*,[4] claims that the Hebrew word *Zona* can also be translated "innkeeper," and favors that translation because of Rahab's personal qualities. He explains that she managed an inn, and since women did not travel only men would stay there. Verkuyl thinks it possible that all such women were called harlots. D. J. Wiseman suggests that the Hebrew word *Zona* denotes "to act in a friendly way to an enemy" and carries no more stigma than befriending those loyal to an alien power.[5]

As for Rahab's personal qualities, she not only believed in God, but had spiritual discernment to perceive divine leading in the Israelite mission. Verkuyl points out that she was industrious: the flax on her roof had to be prepared, and was later to be transformed into linen and oilwicks. Moreover, she was close to her family - parents, siblings, and their mates and children; their safety was uppermost in her mind.

Her devotion to her family was evidently reciprocated, for she assumed they trusted her enough to accept sanctuary in her house, and would not hesitate to bring their children into the inn. In other words, she was accepted as a family member - a status not usually accorded a prostitute.[6]

Finally, Rahab is named by Matthew as the wife of a leading member of the community. All this is inconsistent with the tradition that Rahab was a harlot. In any event, through faith and repentance, her life was touched and changed by the Divine drama in which she played a prominent role.

Sarah, the widow of Zarephath, the Shunammite woman, and Rahab are not the only women in the eleventh chapter of Hebrews. There are others, although their presence is not immediately obvious.

J. Rendel Harris, a scholar supportive of Harnack's thesis, identified Judith, in the Apocrypha, as the person who "won strength out of weakness, became mighty in war, (and) put foreign armies to flight" (Heb. 11:34).[7] Harris points out that each clause in that section of Hebrews refers to a specific individual or group in the Bible; for example, "stopped the mouths of lions" certainly refers to Daniel.

Harris demonstrates that Clement of Rome, the first century writer who follows Hebrews very closely, automatically identifies Judith with Heb. 11:34. For example, Clement, tracking Hebrews, writes:

> Many women were made strong by the grace of God.

The parallel phrase in Hebrews is:

> out of weakness were made strong.

Again, Clement writes:

> performed manly deeds;

The corresponding phrase in Hebrews:

> waxed valiant in fight (or, "became mighty in war").

Judith, a devout woman, beseeched God in prayer for strength to defeat the Assyrians. She prayed "Give to me, a widow, the strong hand to do what I plan" Judith 9:9). Then, still aware of her weakness, she prayed "Give me strength today, O Lord God of Israel!" (Judith 13:7, NRSV). Her valiant deed was killing the Assyrian general Holofernes by the sword - a course of action not typical of a woman, thus "manly."

Clement writes:

> Judith went forth to the camp of the aliens.

Hebrews has:

> turned back camps of the aliens (or, in another translation, "put foreign armies to flight").

The foreign army put to flight in this instance is that of the Assyrians. Upon discovering the death of Holofernes, they fled in panic (Judith 15:2,3).

As a matter of fact, Clement brings in the name of another woman - Esther - in the category of exemplars of faith, in these words:

> To no less peril did Esther also, who was perfect in faith, expose herself that she might deliver the twelve tribes of Israel, when they were on the point to perish.[8]

Harris comments that the allusion to Esther, following Judith, with such terminology as "perfection in faith," reminiscent of Hebrews, suggests that Esther is to be found in the roll of heroes. Perhaps "escaped the edge of the sword" (Heb. 11:34) might cover the case, Harris says. In Esther 4:11 we are told that there was no escape for anyone who approached the king unbidden by the "golden scepter" (or sword), yet Esther did escape.

There's more. We find in Hebrews language imitative of the apocryphal book, IV Maccabees, in all likelihood the last book in the author's Bible. Such language as "they went about in skins of sheep and goats...they wandered in dense mountains and in caves..." is an echo of II Macc 10:6: "...they had been wandering in the mountains and caves like wild animals."

What does this have to do with female heroes of faith? The Book of Maccabees is concerned with praise for the mother and her seven sons who underwent martyrdom rather than renounce their faith. The sons were exhorted by the mother to hold fast to their faith and were tortured and killed; the mother then committed suicide.

The author of Maccabees wrote: "They vindicated their nation, looking to God and enduring torture even to death" (4 Macc 16:10). Does that sound familiar to you? It should. Just as these witnesses persevered in their faith looking to God and resisting to the point of shedding their blood, we are to "run with perseverance the race that is set before us, looking to Jesus the pioneer and perfecter of our faith...who endured the cross...you have not yet resisted to the point of shedding blood" (Heb. 12:1-4).

To sum up so far, we have named or identified the following women in the eleventh chapter of Hebrews: Sarah, Rahab, the widow of Zarephath, the Shunammite woman, Judith, Esther, and the mother of seven sons. Before we leave this chapter, we need to talk about the first named female hero of faith, Sarah. *A controversy has evolved around the place of Sarah in the roll-call, and certain issues need to be resolved.*

The verse in question is Heb. 11:11. In the RSV it reads:

> By faith Sarah herself received power to conceive, even when she was past the age, since she considered him faithful who had promised.

This verse follows three sentences in which Abraham's faith is described as follows:

> By faith Abraham obeyed when he was called to go out to a place...By faith he sojourned in the land of promise, as in a foreign land...For he looked forward to the city which has foundations, whose builder...is God.

Immediately following, is the verse "By faith Sarah herself..." The feminine pronoun "herself" is intensive - that is, the pronoun is unnecessary and used for emphasis. In the simplest, most straightforward construal of this sentence, Sarah is in the nominative case, that is, she is the subject. Some commentators, however, claim that Abraham is the subject, not Sarah, making him alone an exemplar of faith in this series of sentences. In the NRSV Abraham has supplanted Sarah as a model of faith in the text and Sarah - as a model of faith - has been relegated to a footnote.

Harold W. Attridge., the author of a recent comprehensive commentary on Hebrews, states that standing against any attempt to read Sarah as the subject of Heb. 11:11 is "*the fact that the Sarah of Genesis is not a believer but an amused skeptic.*"[9] The second objection is that the context favors Abraham as the subject.

Consider the first objection to Sarah as a model of faith: she is not a worthy, or logical example. (One is at a loss to explain how the author of Hebrews could deem Rahab a logical model of faith, but not Sarah).

Remember, we are constructing a psychological portrait of the author. If Sarah is in fact a dubious example, we must say the author is willing to overlook her failures, and see her in a favorable light. Perhaps a woman, more likely than a man, would overlook Sarah's initial skepticism. After all, virtually no commentators have done so in the past.

Or perhaps the author took a second look at Sarah's skepticism, for a different perspective, and the time has come for us to do the same.

The incident that underlies this discussion is found in the 18th chapter of Genesis. Three supernatural messengers tell Abraham that Sarah will conceive and bear a son. Sarah overhears their conversation and being past age for childbearing, laughs to herself. So far *no one has said anything directly to her* and unlike Abraham, she has had no opportunity to evaluate the authority or supernatural charisma of the messengers. In fact Sarah was not even asked why she laughed, but the question was put to Abraham: “Why did Sarah laugh...?” Apparently when Sarah was finally able to evaluate the messenger she was in awe and frightened, and in her fear she denied laughing.

So then, shall we dismiss Sarah as “an amused skeptic”? Not yet.

Now consider the 17th chapter of Genesis (v. 15-17). “God said to Abraham” - this was no indirect message from a trio of visitors, but a revelation from heaven: “God said to Abraham, 'As for Sarah your wife...I will bless her, and moreover I will give you a son by her. I will bless her, and she shall give rise to nations; kings of peoples shall come from her'.” Before we dismiss Sarah whom God twice promised to bless - observe how *Abraham* responded to the Divine promise:

> Then Abraham fell on his face and laughed. (Gen. 17:17)

Please visual this! In the Revised English Bible we have this translation: “Abraham bowed low, and laughing said to himself...” Now, when God appeared to Abraham to make a covenant (Gen. 17:3) we find the same translation: “Abram bowed low.”

When we read in v. 17 that he bowed low, we might have the impression that Abraham was rendering obeisance, humbling himself. But that was not the case.

We can see more clearly what was happening in the NRSV translation of Gen. 17:17: "Then Abraham fell on his face and laughed, and said to himself..." Abraham was bent over double because he was convulsed with laughter! An even worse scenario is that he dissembled, bowing before God but laughing in his heart at the Divine revelation.

In either case, we should ask: why does the world remember Sarah's subdued laughter, which she soon repented, fearful because she *did* believe - why does the world remember Sarah's laughter and hold her culpable for it, and forget that Abraham fell on his face quite overcome with mirth?

Now let's go back to the question: Is Sarah a reasonable model of faith? Why not? Did Sarah's initial disbelief outweigh Abraham's? Did she outlaugh him? And yet, one commentator remarks, "it...is a generous interpretation of the text to assume Sarah ... (acted) by faith."[10]

Perhaps *this* is what we should add to the author's psychological profile: generosity in evaluating the spiritual role of Sarah in her nation's history - seeing her intrinsic faithfulness instead of her momentary confusion and disbelief. In this sense, the author was a "feminist."

The second objection to Sarah as the subject of Heb. 11:11 centers around the phrase translated variously as follows:

> was enabled to conceive (NEB)
> received power to conceive (RS)
> received power of procreation (NRSV)

Those who believe the text requires the translation "received power of procreation" argue that Abraham is more logically the subject of the sentence. To that assumption there are several rebuttals. The first is that the words translated "was enabled to conceive" can be translated "was enabled to found a posterity," and this alternative translation is entirely justifiable. It is justifiable linguistically - as Greek lexicons will confirm - and *in context.*

In the sentence immediately preceding the one in question, Abraham is said to have looked forward to a city with foundations whose architect and builder is God. In the next sentence, Sarah was enabled to found a posterity in fulfillment of God's promise. According to one commentator:

> ...the author may have intentionally compared the two. On the one hand, there was the city which had the foundations, which was the capital of the nation; and, on the other hand, there was Isaac, the "foundation" of the chosen people, the seed of Abraham, who were destined to be heirs of the land of the promise (11:9) and the city which had the foundations (11:10).[11]

Even if we do not posit the translation "was enabled to found a posterity"; even if we use the translation "received power of procreation," or, "received power to conceive," as in the RSV, or, literally "to conceive seed," the author's use of idiomatic language can still apply to Sarah.[12]

In fact, if we insist on making Abraham the subject of Heb. 11:11, we have to explain why he, rather than Sarah is past the age of fertility - or, as in some manuscripts, past the age for childbearing.

Let's take another look at Heb. 11:11 and see what happens when we try to make Abraham the subject of the sentence. As we have seen, this occurs in the NRSV. We read "By faith he (Abraham) received power of procreation, even though he was too old..." Now, the Greek text reads "past the normal time of age," or idiomatically, "past the age of fertility," and several manuscripts have "past the time of age *for childbearing*." Several manuscripts even have "She gave birth," that is, "She gave birth past the normal time of age." The reading "too old" for "past the age for childbearing" or "past the normal age" certainly loses something in translation! The effect, of course, is to establish Abraham as the subject.

There is another matter to consider. If Sarah is not in the nominative case, and the subject of the sentence, then just what is she grammatically? Attridge. assigns the dative case to "Sarah herself," or in some manuscripts "barren Sarah herself". The dative requires an iota subscript, which would not have been indicated, and must be assumed. Attridge translates the phrase "Sarah herself though barren" or "Barren Sarah herself" as follows: "With Sarah's involvement." Another translator suggests that the reference to Sarah is a circumstantial clause and gives the reading: "By faith, even though Sarah was sterile, he (Abraham...)". Notice that the intensive pronoun, "herself" in the phrase "Sarah herself" has simply been dropped. Alternate translations become increasingly odd, with one proposal to treat "Sarah herself" as a "dative of advantage," with the reading, "It is by faith that, to the benefit of Sarah herself, he (Abraham)..."

The description of Sarah as sterile or barren is found in a number of important manuscripts including P46. We can translate: "Sarah herself though barren" or "barren Sarah herself." If Sarah though (previously) barren was enabled to found a posterity, we have a logical juxtaposition of thought. If Abraham was enabled to found a posterity though Sarah was barren, we have an awkward sentence construction and a problematical reference to his being past the age for reproduction.

If instead of translating "found a posterity" we translate "procreate" or "conceive seed" and Abraham is the subject, we must ask what essential difference does it make if Sarah was barren? Abraham, though old, could have fathered a child who fulfilled God's promise, through faith, whether or not Sarah had been barren. The reference to Sarah's barrenness is somewhat gratuitous and detracts from Abraham as the protagonist. Furthermore it results in a circumlocution - "By faith he was enabled, though he was past the right age, and though Sarah was barren..."

There are other stylistic problems in making Abraham the subject. Word order is flexible in Greek, but there are logical limits. The translation in the NRSV rearranges word order leaving only "By faith" and the last clause in place. Consider how forced it is to translate: "By faith he received power of procreation, even though he was past the right age - and Sarah herself was barren." Compare with the smooth flow of words in the following translation: "By faith Sarah herself though barren was enabled to found a posterity..." and decide which choice is awkward and which is elegant, in conformity with the style of Hebrews.

In summary, there is no compelling reason to presume iota subscripts making "Sarah herself" dative. Closest adherence to the text, evidence for the reference to childbearing past normal age, and stylistic considerations secure the place of Sarah as subject of Heb. 11:11 and a model of faith.

In our search for the author of Hebrews, again, we must envision how the author thought about Sarah - and go beyond the conventional view that Sarah fell from grace by laughing at the revelation of God. The author of Hebrews knew, as all believers must know, that temporary doubt, fear and denial can be transmuted into steadfast faith. If this were not so, what hope would there be for any of us in our spiritual pilgrimage?

The author's perception of Sarah may differ from own in yet another way. We know Sarah as a Hebrew matriarch. However, Savina Teubal, a researcher in ancient Near Eastern studies, suggests that Sarah had previously been a Mesopotamian priestess, who at one time did not plan to have a biological descendant.[13] Thus Sarah was a more complex personage with higher spiritual standing than is apparent to us.

There is one more woman who is mentioned, though not by name, in the roll call of heroes of faith. In Heb. 11:23 we read: "By faith Moses was hidden by his parents (his mother as well as his father) for three months after his birth, because they saw that the child was beautiful; and they were not afraid of the king's edict" (NRSV). The story is told in Ex. 2:1-4, and in Exodus the mother acts alone - making the decision, preparing the papyrus basket, and placing the basket on the river bank, while the baby's sister stood watch. In the Septuagint or Greek Old Testament - the author's Bible - both parents are credited with hiding the baby for three months. Note, however, that in the Septuagint it is the mother alone who performed the actual deed of saving the infant: "And when they could no longer hide him, his mother took for him an ark, and besmeared it with bitumen, and cast the child into it, and put it in the ooze by the river." (Ex. 2:3).

And to reiterate, it is in this chapter that we find the sympathetic reference to Pharaoh's daughter.

Why are there so many women in the eleventh or "Heroes of Faith" chapter of the Epistle to the Hebrews? This is a pertinent question, and an obvious answer is that a woman wrote it. Still, some people ask why more women are not included - women such as Deborah and Huldah. J. Rendel Harris wrote: "...there ought to be no hesitation in saying...that the eleventh chapter has feminized...if this be correct, the case for the authorship of Priscilla is much strengthened...We are still somewhat surprised at not finding a definite reference to Deborah, but what we have found is positive evidence, which silence on certain points hardly affects any further."[14]

I am inclined to agree with Harris that weighty evidence exists for the inclusion of women in the catalogue of Heroes of Faith in Hebrews. Indeed, their prominence is remarkable. The exclusion of one woman or another should have no bearing on the conclusions we draw.

Gilbert Bilezikian discerns a reference to the ministry of three additional women in the eleventh chapter. Although the women themselves are not in the Catalogue of Heroes, their contribution to religious history is encompassed. He finds in verse 32 that three pairs of names have been inverted chronologically so that the more important personage is named first. The pairs are: Gideon and Barak; Samson and Jephthah; and David and Samuel. The lesser individuals, in each case, paved the way, or set a precedent for the more dominant one. Bilezikian notes that each of the lesser individuals was indebted to a woman for his place in history.

Bilezikian writes:

> Barak owed his victory to Deborah (Judg. 4-5), Jephthah to his daugher's sacrifice (Judge. 11), and Samuel owed his ministry to the dedication of his mother Hannah (1 Sam. 1)...Indeed, by resorting to the subtle device of name inversions, the author of Hebrews seems to convey the message that God used the discreet ministries of women singularly chosen by Him to bring about history-shaping deliverances by the hand of Gideon, Samson, and David.[15]

Bilezikian believes that references to women in the eleventh chapter "illustrate the causalities of sacred history." For example, Sarah originated the people of God, Rahab facilitated their entry into the promised land, and Hannah, through Samuel, was contributory to the rise of David.[16] He goes on to say that the very subtlety with which the theme is developed "suggests the restrained hand of a woman."

Before we leave this part of our discussion it might be appropriate to consider the naming of Jephthah as a Hero of Faith. Some people believe that his sacrifice of his daughter did not qualify him for inclusion in the Roll Call of Heroes of Faith, and a woman author of the epistle, in particular, would not include him.

There are a couple of possible replies to this objection to Priscilla's authorship. First, the author may simply not have thought of the sacrifice of Jephthah's daughter in that context, but may have regarded it as sacrifice that secured Jephthah's victory. The other reply is that Jephthah did not in fact kill his daughter, but sacrificed her in the sense of dedicating her to the Temple.

Solomon Landers, writing in *Bible Review* ("Did Jephthah Kill His Daughter?"), argues it was more than likely Jephthah's vow was modified, and his daughter was not killed. The burning of sons and daughters was explicity forbidden in Israelite law, and deemed abhorrent. Thus Jephthah's vow was illegal and could have been annulled by payment of a fine. Since the daughter, as a human and as a female, was not acceptable as a "burnt offering," she could have been otherwise dedicated.

Landers believes that Jepthah's daughter was sacrificed in the sense of being dedicated to Temple as a caretaker, to live out her life in perpetual virginity, perhaps in solitary confinement. He notes that in various Bible translations, she was lamented, commemorated, had dirges chanted for her, or was talked to by the daughters of Israel (Judges 11:40).[17] Some Rabbinic writers record that she was visited four days a year to be spoken to and consoled by the daughters of Israel.[18]

Landers goes on to say that the superb assessment of Jephthah by the author of Hebrews, as well as the author of Samuel, indicates that both agree with him that Jephthah's daughter was not slain, but consigned "to an isolated life as a virgin."

In summation, the presence of women is pervasive in the eleventh chapter of Hebrews. Their influence is in all cases noble, their deeds essential in God's providential activity, their faith a touchstone.

We Discuss a Controversial Participle: Was the Author a Female?

At this point in our argument we have amassed considerable evidence that the author of Hebrews was feminine in outlook, interests, and style of expression. There can be little doubt that the role of women in religious history is prominently displayed, directly and by allusion. This is an appropriate time to discuss a certain Greek participle that some commentators claim is a disqualifying obstacle to female authorship.

The writer of Hebrews used the idiomatic phrase "time would fail me in telling..." (Heb. 11:32). The Greek word for "telling" is διηγούμενον (transliterated *diegoumenon).* Now, someone has said the use of the participle *diegoumenon* "strongly militates against" the theory that Priscilla wrote it. Reasons? First, the participle is masculine. Second, a female author could have said the same thing in many other ways, avoiding the participle, if she wanted to conceal who she was.[19]

Since many commentators have seized upon this participle to disqualify Priscilla, a rebuttal is clearly in order.

In Greek, all present and future passive participles are declined like adjectives. They agree in gender with the noun or pronoun they refer to. In this phrase, "telling," refers to the pronoun "me." These are the endings in the first person singular:

_____μεν(ος) (masculine gender)

_____μεν(η) (feminine gender)

_____μεν(ον) (neuter gender)

It is important to be aware that in the text, masculine and neuter forms of the participle are identical, and *the feminine differs by a single letter.*

We must consider the following possibilities:

First - the participle was originally feminine, and with slight modification, it was altered to protect the epistle from rejection when copies were circulated from Rome years later.

Second - the participle was originally feminine and was altered as deliberate suppression of the author's identity at a time when female leadership in the church was out of favor.

Peake is one scholar who suspects the word ending may have been feminine at first. If it were, someone was sure to eye it balefully and make it masculine. *Changing a single letter* would do it.

Is there doubt in anyone's mind that a single letter could have been altered to change the author's identity? Consider the comparable fate of Nympha in Col. 4:15. We read of greetings to Nympha and the church that meets at *her* house in RSV and Rev. English Bible, but Nympha has undergone a metamorphosis in the KJV and New American Bible, where greetings are sent to *Nymphas* and the church that meets in *his* house.

In Rom. 16:7 there is similar disagreement over *Junia* who is a *woman* of note among the apostles also known as *Junias,* a *man* of note among the apostles. Is the person in question a man or a woman? We know that Junia was a common feminine name, but the masculine form cannot be documented. Some manuscripts even have "Julia." Junia was assumed to be a woman by *all* commentators - John

Chrysostom, Origen, Jerome, and others, until the thirteenth century when Aegidius of Rome decided otherwise.[20]

Changing a single letter led to a change of gender for Nympha and Junia. Even Priscilla was not immune from masculinization of her name. An ancient Syriac document links "Priscus and Acquilas," Priscus being the masculine form of "Prisca."[21] This, despite her identification as Aquila's wife in Acts 18:2.

The possibility that the participle in Heb. 11:32, *diegoumenon*, was altered cannot be disregarded.

Peake is not the only scholar who thought this occurred. J. Rendel Harris thought there might be a manuscript with the feminine participle although he did not succeed in locating one. There is ample evidence that the so-called "Western" text of Acts underwent changes to reduce the pre-eminence of Priscilla, and this may be another example of the trend.[22]

There is another possibility. Friends of Priscilla may have used a masculine word ending to cloak her identity when the letter was copied and circulated years later, although her identity was, of course, known to the original recipients. That is, the document was altered to protect it amidst growing disapproval of women teachers and leaders. This differs from deliberate suppression, because the motive is different.

Or it may be, as Harnack intimated, that "time will fail me in telling" is a *literary plural form*. The author of Hebrews characteristically reverts from first person singluar to first person plural. The literary plural form appears elsewhere in Hebrews:

> Heb. 2:5 "of which WE are speaking"
> Heb. 5:11 "about this WE have much to say", and
> Heb. 9:5 - in which the pronoun is actually lacking "of these things
> WE cannot now speak in detail" (lack of time, as in Heb. 11:32?)

A female author may have wished to use the idiom "time will fail me (us) in telling," which is transitional in leading to the next section, and used the singular form in 11:32 *to vary her phraseology* from the plural form in 2:5, 5:11 and 9:5.

Our author customarily uses different expressions for the sake of variety, according to Ellingworth and Nida, specialists in the translation of Hebrews. The writer of Hebrews is a "literary craftsman," according to them, for whom stylistic considerations outweigh "precise differences of meaning."[23]

Thus, if 11:32 were intended as a literary plural, the use of the masculine participle is explained. Bilezikian believes that Priscilla, as a woman, was mindful of some limitations to her status and in this perspective, the gender of the participle *diegoumenon* "need not be anything more than an editorial masculine."[24]

Either scenario is plausible: (1) the participle was a literary plural form, or (2) the participle was originally feminine and a single letter was changed to suppress the author's identify.

From there it was inevitable that the name of the author should be mysteriously and inexplicably "lost."

NOTES TO CHAPTER IV

1. J. B. Lightfoot, tr. and ed., completed by J. R. Harmer "The Epistle of S. Clement to the Corinthians," *The Apostolic Fathers*, Grand Rapids: Baker Book House, 1970, p. 18.
2. The Rev. Prof. A. T. Hanson, "Rahab the Harlot in Early Christian Tradition," JSNT I (1978)53-60.
3. Lane, *op. cit.*, Vol. 47B, p. 369.
4. G. Verkuyl, "The Berkeley Version of the N.T.," BT 2 (1951) 84-85. (*Bible Translator*).
5. Lane, *op. cit.*, p. 379, citing D.J. Wiseman, "Rahab of Jericho," TynBul 14 (1964) 8-11.
6. Lane, *op. cit.*, p. 379.
7. James Rendel Harris, Lecture V, "Sidelights on the Authorship of the Epistle of the Hebrews," *Sidelights on New Testament Research* (London: The Kingsgate Press, James Clarke & Co., 1908), p. 169-171.
8. Lightfoot, *op. cit.*, p. 36.
9. Harold W. Attridge., *A Commentary on the Epistle to the Hebrews* (Hermeneia - A Critical and Historical Commentary on the Bible) (Phil.: Fortress Press, 1989), p. 325.
10. Buchanan, *op. cit.*, p. 190.
11. *Ibid.*
12. Lane, *op. cit.*, Vol. 47B, p. 345.
13. Savina Teubal's book is *Sarah the Priestess - The First Matriarch of Genesis* (Athens, OH: Swallow Press, 1984).
14. Harris, *op. cit.*, p. 174.
15. Bilezikian, *op. cit.*, p. 303-304.
16. *Ibid.*, p. 304.
17. Solomon Landers, "Did Jephthah Kill His Daughter?" *Bible Review*, Aug., '91, Vol. VII No. 4, p. 28-31, 42.
18. *Ibid.*, citing Shoshanah, *Derekh Binah,* p. 177.
19. H. T. Andrews, "Hebrews," *The Abingdon Bible Commentary*, p. 1297-8.
20. Paul R. Smith, *Is it Okay to Call God "Mother" Considering the Feminine Face of God* (Peabody, Mass: Hendrickson Publishers, 1993), p. 112, n.12 citing Aegidius, *Opera Exegetica,* Opuscula I in *Journal of Biblical Equality*

(July 1992)44. See also: Comfort, *op. cit.*, p. 137; Ben Witherington III, *Women in the Earliest Churches* (Cambridge: University Press, 1988), p. 114-115; and James D. G. Dunn, "Romans 9-16," *Word Biblical Commentary,* Vol. 38 (Dallas: Word Books, 1988), p. 894.

21. Cureton, William. tr., *Ancient Syriac Documents Relative to the Earliest Establishment of Christianity in Edessa and the Neighboring Countries. Preface by W. Wright*. Amsterdam: Oriental Press, 1967), p. 35. See note, p. 173, citing "Priscilla" in two other manuscripts.

22. Harnack; also Ben Witherington, "Antifeminist tendencies of the 'Western' text in Acts," JBL 103:1 (1984) 82-4.

23. Ellingworth and Nida, *op. cit.*, p. 2.

24. Bilezikian, *op. cit.*, p. 303.

CHAPTER FIVE

WE VIEW THE LINE-UP

Imagine that we have been summoned to view a line-up of possible authors. There is no shortage of "suspects." From left to right, we scan the field. First we see Paul reluctantly holding a placard with the word "Author." He has been there a long time and appears relieved when someone divests him of the placard. We focus momentarily on Clement of Rome, whose innocent mien deflects our attention. Next is Barnabas, apprehended in a third century dragnet to capture a suspect. We pause. He looks guilty but he has a string of alibis. To his right is distinguished Apollos - a relative newcomer, whose presence is credited to Luther. Apollos is to be scrutinized and ultimately dismissed, then shadowed, for he will lead us to the real author.

An unfamiliar figure is puzzling. His name is Aristion, and at first we don't know why he is there. Later we find out that he represents himself and other minor suspects, as well as the hypothetical "unknown person." Near the end of the line is Aquila, a recent arrival, and finally Priscilla, the newest arrival of all, and by coincidence a woman.

The purpose of a line-up is to identify a person or persons, and to weed out and dismiss others who are under suspicion. The purpose of this chapter is to eliminate candidates for the authorship of Hebrews, one by one, until Priscilla stands alone.

Arthur Conan Doyle, creator of the Sherlock Holmes detective stories, said: "When you have eliminated the impossible, whatever remains, however improbable, must be the truth." (Not that a female author of scripture is improbable - although for some it will take some getting used to.) Once the negative case for Priscilla's authorship of Hebrews is established, positive evidence will be adduced showing that she had means, motive and opportunity. Then I present an hypothesis, based on certain known facts, surmising how and when she had occasion to write the letter. This, in general, is the procedure. Step-by-step, weight of evidence will accrue for Harnack's theory.

Paul: A Ghostly Presence

From late antiquity to the Renaissance, Paul was widely accepted as the author,[1] a viewpoint now generally regarded as indefensible. We have already remarked on the irreconcilable difference in style, and disavowal of apostolic status in the author's conversion story.

There used to be a theory that Paul wrote the epistle in Hebrew and someone translated it into Greek. Clement of Alexandria argued that Luke was the translator;[2] Eusebius concurs with Pauline authorship but prefers Clement of Rome as the translator. We don't know why this view gained currency. "Time will fail me in telling" is not the only Greek idiom in the epistle. There are many compound Greek words with no Aramaic equivalent.[3] Quotations from the Old Testament are from the Greek Septuagint.[4] Stately elegance of style argues against the translation theory.

Then we must ask: if Paul were the author, why didn't he sign his name? Clement of Alexandria has an explanation: Paul was an apostle to the Gentiles. He was too modest to go outside his province to be an apostle to the Hebrews as well.[5]

What wonderful nonsense! Paul's apostleship was from the Lord. If God led him to write to the Hebrews, Paul would have affixed his name and claimed God's inspiration. If not, Paul would have left the epistle unwritten.

In 1939, William Leonard bravely tried to show that Paul was the author, but even he admitted Paul did not write the epistle in its final form.[6]

Though Paul no longer bears the appellation "Author of Hebrews," he remains a ghostly presence in the epistle. Paul's manner of speaking and theological concerns are interwoven in its fabric, though filtered through the medium of a distinctive and original mind. The author of Hebrews was closely associated with Paul, engaging in many hours of conversation with him. No candidate for authorship can be considered who does not fit this description.

Clement of Rome - Spokesman for Ecclesiastical Law and Order

Clement looks innocent enough in the line-up but he was actually identified as the author by Hippolytus early in the third century.[7] Calvin voted for two candidates, unable to choose between Luke and Clement.[8] Eusebius favored him as "translator", finding "similar phraseology" in Hebrews and Clement's letter. He also notes the "absence of differing outlook."[9] Both reasons are subject to dispute.

Ostensibly, Clement is neither the author nor the translator. Of prominent suspects Clement, Barnabas and Apollos, who is least likely to be the author? In this three-way contest of improbability, Clement is a cinch to win.

Exactly who was Clement of Rome? He is not to be confused with Clement of Alexandria, who thought Paul was the author of Hebrews. To identify him with Paul's co-worker, Clement, in Philippians 4:35 is only an uninformed guess.

Clement was a presbyter-bishop in Rome who, in 96 or 97 A.D., wrote a letter to the Corinthian church. We have seen that Eusebius, the third century church historian, comparing this letter with the epistle to the Hebrews, found what he regarded as striking similarities. Where Clement quotes and echoes Hebrews, we expect to find similar phraseology. Closer inspection reveals that in style and outlook the letters are drastically different.

Hebrews was widely circulated by the time Clement's letter was written. Clement assumed the Corinthians knew it well. No need to identify the source of his quotations - much less, to name the author - assuming that he knew the author's name and there were a reason to allow it to fade into oblivion.

In chapters nine though twelve of his own letter, Clement expatiated on Heroes of Faith delineated in Heb. 11:4-40.[10] Does this mean he wrote Hebrews? He also discoursed on the resurrection in chapter 24, enlarging on I Cor. 15:12-57. He warned against factions in chapter 47, adding to I Cor. 3:3-11. He even paraphrased Paul's hymn on love:

> Love puts up with everything and is always patient. There is nothing vulgar about love, nothing arrogant. Love knows nothing of schism or revolt. Love does everything in harmony. By love all God's elect were made perfect. Without love nothing can please God (Clement 49 5).[11]

Surely these words are reminiscent of I Cor. 13:1-13. Did Clement therefore write I Corinthians? Of course not. Did he write the epistle to the Hebrews because he imitated its eleventh chapter? No.

The two letters diverge in level of artistry and degree of religious exaltation, testifying to different authorship. Consider matters of style. When faced with two words of like meaning, the frugal author of Hebrews was likely to use one and save the other. With monotonous predictability, Clement used both.

Clement begins redundantly:

> Due, dear friends, to the *sudden and successive misfortunes and accidents* we have encountered, we have, we admit, been rather long in *turning* our attention to your quarrels. We refer to the *abominable and unholy* schism, so *alien and foreign* to those whom God has chosen, which a few *impetuous and headstrong* fellows have fanned to such a pitch of insanity that your good name, once so *familiar and dear* to us all, has fallen into the gravest ill repute (Clement 1:1)[12]

He continues with characteristic wordiness:

> By reason of *rivalry and envy the greatest and most righteous* pillars...(Clement 5:2).

> Thoughtless, silly, senseless and ignorant...(Clement 39:1)

and heads for a verbose ending:

> ...Peace, harmony, and stability...(Clement 61:1).

Do we find the same usage in Hebrews? We do not. The unrestrained use of synonyms is peculiar to Clement. In Hebrews, the author uses words sparingly - with telling effect.

Read the two letters. Note the enormous differences in style. Balance the long discourses of Clement against the concise logic of Hebrews. Then see how they clash in point of view.

The one who wrote Hebrews drew upon abundance of spiritual fervor to transform the apathy of his - or her - readers. They ought to imitate their leaders! They are to grow in mind and spirit! Through Christ, their High Priest, the way to Heaven is open!

The author of Hebrews gloried in the spirit of early Christianity; Clement was temperamentally different. Dealing with inspired laypersons at odds with their uninspired leaders, his plea was: "Don't rock the boat." Ecclesiastical officeholders were being deposed. According to Clement, they must be obeyed, although people thought God was leading them. Led by the Spirit, people wanted to speak. Clement deflated them: they weren't so eloquent after all, he said: they stir up trouble, and lack humility.

To Clement, order and docility are the quintessence of Christian faith. Richardson detects a movement away from Pauline religion to a routinized concern for ethics and law.[13] Thirty years had gone by since Paul and the writer of Hebrews reminded the church that spiritual gifts are of God, who is free to bestow them.[14] The apostles were gone.[15] The church at Corinth was ancient and solid. *Now* when God kindled a flame the church was apt to pour buckets of water over it. If Clement were the author of both letters, he turned 180 degrees in outlook.

In style and standpoint, Clement and the author of Hebrews are miles apart. Then too, Clement never had an identifiable ministry to Hebrew Christians, nor does he meet certain other specifications for authorship. As for the other notion that he might have been the "translator," we do not envy Eusebius the task of revealing that Hebrews was not written in Greek.

Barnabas - Apostle to the Gentiles

In first century Alexandria, Christians treasured a letter urging them to adhere to their faith. Title: "The Epistle of Barnabas to the Hebrews."[16] So recorded Tertullian, about 200 A.D. Tertullian preferred Barnabas as the author (without ever telling why), placing him in the line-up. Several modern scholars concur.[17]

Why was the name Barnabas affixed to the title of Hebrews in certain manuscripts? For the same reason Paul's name is affixed to the title in the King James and other Bibles. Either of these men would be warmly welcomed as authors. Though not one of the Twelve, Barnabas had apostolic status.[18] Leadership of the church was his before it became Paul's. The name of one or the other of these men was sure to enhance the letter's acceptability.

Now, in the second century another letter was circulated in North Africa - not as well-written, but on a similar theme. Someone named Barnabas wrote it.[19] Clement of Alexandria said it was by Paul's companion, Barnabas. (Like Tertullian, Clement wrote about 200 A.D.) But today it is known as the work of a Jewish Christian of Alexandria, most likely dating from 135-150 A.D.[20] The title was "The Epistle of Barnabas."[21]

So in the third century two epistles, written about 70 years apart, bore the name of Barnabas. One came into the New Testament as "The Letter to the Hebrews." The later one remained apocryphal, as "The Epistle of Barnabas".[22] Paul's companion, Barnabas, did not write either one.

Even the earliest theories of authorship (Paul, Luke, Barnabas, Clement of Rome) sprang up years after Hebrews was written.[23] Tertullian's theory naming Barnabas was no exception, and equally false. First, I will show how the apocryphal "Epistle of Barnabas" differs from the letter to the Hebrews, and why it must have been written later, by someone else. Then I will explain why I think Barnabas died before New Testament "Hebrews" was written. At the last we will see that Barnabas couldn't have written Hebrews even if had lived to be one hundred years old.

Inferior in style and religious insight, filled with error and trivia,[24] the apocryphal letter of Barnabas is not an appealing document. This may be why no one credited (or blamed) the Apostle Barnabas for it until Clement of Alexandria, at least fifty years after it was composed.

Think of Barnabas, a Levite, who helped in Temple worship, described in the Bible as a man of faith and goodness. Recall how he sought out Paul, when many Christians distrusted him, and later took second place to him graciously. Then read the so-called "Epistle of Barnabas". Note the many inaccuracies concerning Mosaic law.[25] Did Barnabas the Levite, who knew about Temple worship first-hand, record them? Would a Levite downgrade the Temple, and the sacrifices of the priests? Not so relentlessly, we can be reasonably certain.

See how the letter gloats over the destruction of the Temple.[26] "The Jews trusted in the temple, not in God; through their going to war, it was destroyed by their enemies, just as Jesus said it would be", etcetera. Did Barnabas, with his respect for Judaism, and his generous spirit, write these words? It is even doubtful that he lived to see the destruction of the Temple in 70 A.D.

Barnabas did not write the apocryphal "Epistle of Barnabas" even though it has been ascribed to him. We cannot assume he wrote the Epistle to the Hebrews merely because Tertullian and other said he did, and his name once appeared in the title. No, not without supporting evidence - and such is not forthcoming.

Some people are willing to believe that Barnabas wrote these letters because they describe Jewish worship with superficial similarity. For example, both have something to say about the "rest of God," but further study shows how they diverge. In the apocryphal letter, the "rest of God" is nothing more than the end of his work on the seventh day of creation. To the writer of Hebrews, to enter the rest of God is to take hold of his promises by faith (Heb. 4:3). Warning the readers, the author recounts the disobedience of Israelites who were kept in the wilderness for forty years because of their unbelief.[27] Obedience to God is "being" more than "doing," for God sees the "thoughts and intentions of the heart" (Heb. 4:12) and one has no place to hide from God. Incisiveness marks the letter to the Hebrews; harshness, the "Epistle of Barnabas".

Another point of resemblance is the theme of Temple worship. Actually, Hebrews never mentions the Temple, referring only to the Tabernacle of Old Testament times. Certainly, though the Tabernacle is delineated, the ascendancy of Christian worship is clearly implied. So it is highly unlikely that Hebrews could have been written later than 70 A.D., without alluding to the destruction of the Temple for emphasis - as does the "Epistle of Barnabas". Also, Hebrews 8:4ff implies the Temple was still open for worship and ritual.[28]

Then, the letters were written by different persons, and Barnabas did not write the later one. Did he write the earlier, the Epistle to the Hebrews?

No doubt Barnabas was zealous and authoritative. To attribute Hebrews to him on such a flimsy basis, as some have done,[29] is indefensible.

Many scholars have thought Barnabas to be the author, including Harnack before he opted for Priscilla.[30] Yes, they have superficially plausible reasons. But plausibility is not proof, and Barnabas could not have written the Epistle.

First of all, a Levite is not more likely to have written Hebrews than the "Epistle of Barnabas". We have seen that Hebrews refers to the ancient Tabernacle and not directly to the Temple in Jerusalem, where a Levite would spend much time with his ceremonial chores. Indeed, the author is not familiar with ceremonial procedures, essentially the same for both.[31] Erroneously, the golden censer is said to stand in the Holy of Holies (Heb. 9:4). In fact, the censer stood on the altar in front of the ark (Exodus 40:5). Once a year, on the Day of Atonement, the chief priest brought it inside the veiled ark (Leviticus 16:12). Nor does the High Priest offer daily sacrifices as in Hebrews 7:27. Wikenhauser doubts if Hebrews 7:27 was written by Jerusalem. He also sees in someone who spent much time in it a disparagement of the daily sacrifices of the priests, that one does not expect of a Levite. Then too, Barnabas tended to observe Jewish food taboos (Galatians 2:13), while the author of Hebrews said they never did anyone any good (Heb. 13:9).

There is much more to say about Barnabas.

The man- or woman- who wrote Hebrews had an extraordinary mastery of the Greek language. Granted, Barnabas was a preacher and teacher. But was he trained in rhetoric and fluent in literary Greek? A native of Cyprus, a resident of Jersualem, probably he wasn't.

The epistle to the Hebrews reads well aloud - an indication that the author was eloquent in speech. Such consummate artistry of style was bound to find expression in speech. How revealing that when Paul and Barnabas were together, Paul was the chief spokesman. Two incidents are recorded in Acts, to this effect. Once, Paul and Barnabas were invited to speak in the synagogue in Antioch of Pisidia (Acts 13:14-16). Only Paul spoke. In Lystra: "Barnabas they called Zeus, and Paul, because he was the chief speaker, they called Hermes" (Acts 14:12). Barnabas would undoubtedly have had his say if he were a compelling speaker. By the way, Priscilla fits in here, for she was spoken of by Tertullian as "the holy Prisca, who preached the gospel."[32] (We meet her further along in the line-up and will see how more and more she becomes the prime suspect.)

It is true, as all scholars who vote for Barnabas have shown, that he was of Paul's circle - like the author. But the author, unlike Barnabas, was Timothy's co-worker. Timothy replaced Barnabas as Paul's right-hand man at the beginning of Paul's second missionary journey in 49 or 50 A.D. and remained so to the end of Paul's days (see II Timothy, chapter 4).

Overseeing the church from a prison cell, Paul asked Timothy to get Mark and bring him to Rome (II Tim. 4:11). Mark had been restored to Paul's favor since an earlier dispute over him but where was Barnabas, Mark's cousin and companion? Why didn't Paul even mention his great friend and former co-worker? As a matter of fact, Barnabas had disappeared from scripture, and this is strange considering his apostolic status. Trace the sequence of events. After he and Paul parted in a disagreement about Mark in 49 or 50 A.D., Paul cited Barnabas as a self-supporting apostle in 56 or 57 A.D. (I Cor. 9:5,6). We know Barnabas was still traveling with the Gospel in 60-62 A.D. for Paul asked the Colossians to welcome him if he came to them (Col. 4:10). Mark was then with Paul, but may have returned to Barnabas. We are sure Mark did not stay with Paul, who later asked Timothy to come and to bring Mark with him. Colossians 4:10, dated 62 A.D. at the latest, is the last we hear of Barnabas.

Coulson and Butler say his disappearance from scripture leads us to infer that by 62 A.D. Barnabas must have been dead.[33] According to one tradition, he was martyred at Salamis, in his native Cyprus, in 61 A.D.[34] (He is considered founder of the Cypriot church.) In the final part of this study I will try to reconstruct the events leading to the composition of Hebrews which occurred a few years after Barnabas may be presumed dead.

Of course, we can infer his death, but we cannot prove it, and other evidence must be brought forth to dismiss him from the line-up. Here is the case for dismissal:

1. Despite his Levitical background, Barnabas became - and remained - an apostle to the Gentiles. His bond with Paul very strong at one time - determined his destiny. As early as 53 A.D. Paul reported:

   And when they perceived the grace that was given to me, James and Cephas and John, who were reported to be pillars, gave to me and Barnabas the right hand of fellowship, that we should go to the Gentiles and they to the circumcised (Galatians 2:9).

Paul reminded the Corinthians that he and Barnabas were not a burden to them (I Cor. 9:6). Then in 56 or 57 A.D., Barnabas was well known to the predominantly Gentile church in Corinth. Still later, in 61 A.D. or so, Paul urged the Colossians to welcome Barnabas if he came to them (Col. 4:1,2). The long-standing ministry to Hebrew Christians in one locality, which produced the Epistle to the Hebrews, cannot be fitted in with Barnabas' career.

2. *The conversion story in Hebrews 2:3*[35] *does not fit Barnabas, who resided in Jerusalem and by inference saw and heard Jesus.*

Barnabas was one of the Seventy (or seventy-two) disciples cited in Luke 10:1, according to Clement of Alexandria.[36] No list of the Seventy has ever been found,[37] and Clement of Alexandria may have been wrong. Even so - even if Barnabas had been converted after Pentecost - he spent much time in Jerusalem and may have lived there:

a. His duties as a Levite brought him to the Temple.
b. He owned property in or near Jerusalem, for he sold a field and gave the money to the apostles (Acts 4:36).
c. His cousin Mark, and Mark's family, lived in Jerusalem.

If Barnabas stayed in Jerusalem for the Passover, as he was sure to do, he must have seen and and heard Jesus, disqualifying himself as a candidate for the authorship of Hebrews. He may well have been one of the Seventy, working closely with Jesus for years.

Before we dismiss Barnabas, mark it doubtful that he wrote Heb. 13:24: "Those who come from Italy send you greetings."

Attridge. sums it up concisely: Despite the appeal of Tertullian's suggested author to some scholars, "he is as unlikely as Paul."[38]

Apollos - Why Luther Guessed Wrong

At last we view Apollos, whose presence in the line-up, though belated, has a semblance of plausibility. "Belated" is an accurate description, for, as one commentator states, Apollos as the author of Hebrews is "A supposition never made by any of the ancient churches, and first ventured upon,...by Luther...We have no external evidence in favour of it; no voice of antiquity being raised to testify,..."[39]

The silence of antiquity speaks to us. It reminds us softly that Apollos' apostolic status would have enhanced the acceptability of the letter. It whispers in our ear that his name would not have been lost by the Christian scholars of Alexandria, where New Testament manuscripts were collected, for Alexandria was Apollos' native city.

"A semblance of plausibility" - for Apollos, like the author, was eloquent and erudite.

We need to take a close look at him, because his path crossed with that of Priscilla and Aquila, who are standing next to him.

Apollos strode onto the stage of history in the eighteenth chapter of Acts. When he spoke, his voice rang out with earnestness and authority. Men and women in the synagogue at Ephesus were moved as the newcomer from Alexandria articulated their hope for the coming of a Messiah and the need for repentance (Acts 18:24,25). The man was a spellbinder.

Who was he? Apollos was somewhat of an ideological wanderer. A "Learned Jew," he was once in the mainstream of Jewish thought - a Pharisee, perhaps, or was we would call "orthodox." As such, he had observed the food regulations, at the very least abstaining from pork. Whoever wrote Hebrews said the food taboos never did any one any good spiritually (Heb. 13:9) - a declaration critical of himself as well as the laws, if Apollos were in fact the author.

In his native Alexandria there were other schools of thought in religion and philosophy. Philo's blend of Judaism and Platonism: heathen gods and festivals; the doctrine of a left-wing sect of Jews who settled in Egypt and elsewhere, known as Essenes - all these impinged on his mind. Somewhere along the way he became a follower of John the Baptist, being taught by the Essenes and holding to their particular Messianic faith.

Soon he would find a spiritual home in the church of Jesus Christ, his long-awaited Messiah, where all his courage and persuasiveness would be used to upbuild His church. Who would lead him to faith in Christ? A married couple, Aquila and Priscilla, who heard him speak one fateful day in the synagogue.

After his conversion, Apollos declared Jesus to be the Messiah foretold in the Old Testament. Those who heard him expound on this subject had a choice. They could believe him and remain silent, or they could argue with him and be soundly defeated in public debate (Acts 18:24-28).

Proof of Jesus' messiahship is the theme of the Epistle to the Hebrews. What's more, Apollos was educated in Alexandria, to account for the "Platonism" in the Epistle, and its use of the Greek Septuagint Old Testament. He may have been trained in rhetoric. No wonder Luther and others[40] thought him to be the author, and why we are viewing Apollos in the line-up. There is, however, a credibility gap in their theory, as we have seen, one that will widen even further as we continue our discussion.

We have already mentioned the "silence of antiquity" in regard to Apollos' authorship of Hebrews. Let's analyze it further.

Apollos and Barnabas are in the same boat, for several reasons. One reason is that both had apostolic status. Paul refers to himself and Apollos as colleagues, using the word "apostles" in his discussion of their roles (I Corinthians 4:9). Clement of Rome reinforced Paul's evaluation of Apollos by recalling his outstanding leadership. With high praise for Apollos, he proclaimed him worthy of their past allegiance, even though it had led to factions. He noted that Peter and Paul "endorsed" him.[41]

Since the man was an apostle, why would his letter be written or circulated anonymously, and why would his name be lost? Why would anyone fail to capitalize on his popular appeal and unquestioned leadership? A certain expositor[42] tries to shrug off the mystery by saying the readers forgot to put Apollos' name on the document. We know (and so does he) the name belonged in the prescript. Nor does he explain the mystery away by denying Hebrews is a letter, for it has the usual ending of a letter, with personal greetings in the postscript.

Peake is sure Clement of Rome knew the author when he echoed Hebrews in his Epistle to the Corinthians. Clement never hinted he was quoting Apollos. Peake infers Apollos was not the source of Clement's extensive quotations.[43]

Expositor Hugh Montefiore tried to show Apollos wrote Hebrews to the Corinthian church about 54 A.D. He argues Clement recalled Hebrews to the Corinthians because he knew it was originally written for them. Not so, on both counts.

1. Hebrews was known and used in Africa, Asia and Europe by 96 A.D., when Clement wrote. Some scholars think it was written to Rome, for it was known there very early, and may even have been circulated in Rome first. If Clement had a particular reason for quoting Hebrews, it may well be that some of the men involved in the dispute in Corinth were Hebrew Christians.

2. How could a message so earnestly exhorting the readers against the peril to their souls of apathy and apostasy have been sent to the fast-growing, exuberant Corinthian church of 54 A.D.? As Paul, founder of the Corinthian church, did not arrive in Corinth until 51 A.D., the church was still brand new and brimming with enthusiasm in 54 A.D. Blessed with spiritual gifts in abundance, Corinthian worshippers were sometimes unruly for this very reason. H.V. Morton quotes R. B. Rackham to the effect that "extraordinary enthusiasm gave rise to disorder in worship."[44]

Montefiore's chronology of events rightly call for an early date for Hebrews. But 54 A.D. is a little too early (see also Heb. 13:7), and he is obviously in the wrong church. Montefiore's reasoning is so ingenious and original as to merit further refutation. He finds in the first four chapters of Paul's first letter to the Corinthians a kind of "dialogue" in which Paul replies to the letter to the Hebrews.[45] I will give two of his examples, with my refutation.

Example I. Paul wrote that he fed the Corinthians milk, not meat, for they were not mature Christians (I Cor. 3:2). Montefiore says Paul was referring to the opinion in Hebrews 5:12 that the readers need milk, or elementary doctrine, instead of solid food, or mature doctrine. Paul, he claims, was defending himself against the charge that he had not given the Corinthians proper instruction.

This is my rebuttal: From the context of Hebrews 5:12, it is clear the author himself had instructed the readers in elementary doctrine, and wished to go on to more mature teaching. At any rate, he blames no one but the readers for their failure to grow in their understanding of the faith.

The milk/solid food analogy, though commonplace in their time, does in fact hint at conversational give-and-take. However, Paul and the author of Hebrews make different use of the expression.

Example II. The writer of Hebrews warned of destruction (by burning) if their religion was not fruitful (Heb. 6:8). Paul presumably had this in mind when he wrote that a false superstructure on his foundation would be saved - "but only as through fire" (I Cor. 3:13-15).

Rebuttal: Apollos was the "builder" on Paul's foundation. If Paul was indeed replying to Hebrews 6:8 by warning Apollos of the danger of a false and fruitless ministry, the "dialogue" is nothing less than open hostility. Only if Apollos meant to attack Paul in Heb. 6:8 could such hostility be understood. From the context of I Corinthians, chapters 1-4, we can see Paul accepted Apollos as a valuable colleague. Paul stressed his own role as founder of the Corinthian church only to discourage the factions that grew around leading personalities, including Apollos.

One more point should be made. Montefiore develops his theory on the ground that Apollos and Paul were friends and co-workers. When Timothy, Paul's right-hand man, was (supposedly) "dispatched to Corinth," who but Apollos would be travelling with him? I detect a certain inconsistency in his reasoning. If the first four chapters of I Corinthians are Paul's defense against a letter by Apollos, and certain misunderstandings caused by it, as hypothesized by Montefiore, the two men could not have been friends at the time. Corinthian Christians of 54 A.D. were squared off into rival factions, acclaiming Apollos in one corner and Paul in another. With the factionalism in Corinth at its height, Apollos could not have been travelling with Paul's closest friend, Timothy.

Nor did Apollos join the inner circle around Paul years later - a circle that still included Timothy, Priscilla and Aquila. Paul himself named Aristarchus, Mark and Justus as the only Jewish Christian men working closely with him for the kingdom of God, in 60 or 61 A.D., nearer to the actual date of the writing of Hebrews (see Col. 4:10-11). There is not one shred of evidence that Apollos was of Paul's circle, when the author of Hebrews divulged plans to travel with Timothy (Heb. 13:23), about 65 A.D.

"Echoes" from Hebrews heard by Montefiore in First Corinthians can be better understood as words of Paul later echoed in Hebrews! And who would reflect the thoughts and sometimes the words of Paul, if not Priscilla and Aquila, with whom Paul lived and worked for eighteen months in Corinth, and with whom he worked for three years in Ephesus? Nothing in the New Testament hints at so close an association between Apollos and Paul.

It is time to compare the conversion story in Heb. 2:3 with the conversion of Apollos in Acts 18:24-28. At this point the credibility gap widens to disqualify Apollos. You will recall the author of Hebrews stated he was converted by persons who saw and heard Jesus. *Apollos became a Christian as the result of instruction by Priscilla and Aquila, who did not themselves see and hear Jesus.*

This needs some explanation, for many people are of the opinion Apollos was a Christian when he arrived in Ephesus and began to speak in the synagogue - imperfectly instructed but still a Christian. He wasn't. The key verse is Acts 18:25:

> *He had been instructed in the way of the Lord; and being fervent in spirit, he spoke and taught accurately the things concerning Jesus, though he knew only the baptism of John.*

Now, the first fact I call to your attention has to do with the phrase "concerning Jesus." This sounds as if Apollos spoke about Jesus' life and teachings, as he would if he were then a Christian. However, "Jesus" is only an alternate reading of the word "Lord." The Greek text has "Lord."

We should understand what is meant by "the things concerning the Lord," in light of the phrase "though he knew only the baptism of John." Apollos preached on the messianic hope of the Jews, using messianic prophecies from the Old Testament as his text. These were "the things concerning the Lord"! He was not talking about the life and death of Jesus. Knowledgeable and accurate as far as he went, he came short of confessing Jesus to be the Messiah. He didn't even know about him! So early was it in the missionary expansion of the church that the church in Corinth had just been founded (by Paul), and in parts of the world the gospel of Jesus Christ had not been preached.

Baptism was the first ritual for converts to the new faith. True, baptism was followed by further instruction and in some cases preceded by instruction- but no one could possibly be a confessing Christian who did not even *know* of baptism in the name of Father, Son and Holy Spirit. Apollos, who knew only the baptism of John, was not then a Christian.

Let's talk more about the "baptism of John" and why it was pre-Christian.

John the Baptist had followers in Ephesus (and other places) about fifteen years after his death early in the known career of Jesus. He was thought by some to be the Messiah. (This is why the fourth gospel stressed the inferiority of John the Baptist to Jesus).[46] These persons were affiliated with the Essene sect, with whom John himself had some connection. Among them he had been a non-conformist, but he shared their Messianic expectations. Like the Essenes at Qumran, he preached repentance, to be followed by baptism, in preparation for the coming of the Messiah. The Messiah would then baptize with the Holy Spirit (Matt. 3:1,2,6,11). The Manual of Discipline of the Qumran community demanded repentance before baptism, and promised God would give the Holy Spirit and the "Spirit of Truth as purifying water," when the Messiah came.[47] Then the baptism of John was only preparatory for the coming of the Messiah, and was not the same as Christian baptism.

Here is further proof that the "baptism of John" was pre-Christian.

After Apollos left Ephesus, Paul arrived. He found some "disciples" who like Apollos knew only John's baptism (see Acts 19:1-7. Paul told them:

> *John baptized with the baptism of repentance, telling the people to believe in the one who was to come after him, that is, Jesus (Acts 19:4).*

Obviously, they were John's disciples, not Jesus'. What did Paul do then? He baptized them in the name of the Lord Jesus. If they had been "imperfectly instructed Christians" Paul would not have baptized them again. He'd simply correct their theology! No, they were not Christians, and neither was Apollos a Christian - until Priscilla and Aquila told him of Jesus, the Christ (Acts 18:26-28).

We haven't dismissed Apollos from the line-up yet. How do we know the author of Hebrews *first* heard the word of salvation from those who saw Jesus? Perhaps Apollos - who was converted by Priscilla and Aquila - then received further confirmation from the immediate disciples of Jesus. If so, he could have written

Hebrews 2:3. In other words, is Heb. 2:3 in fact a conversion story? Even though scholars agree that it is, you want to see for yourself:

> *It was declared at first by the Lord, and it was attested to us by those who heard him (Heb. 2:3).*

The keyword is "attested," or "confirmed" as in other translations. The Greek word is ἐβεβαιώθη. It means: confirmed, established, ratified or asserted. This is important: In the *middle voice* βεβαιόω means "to secure for oneself" or "to feel confirmed." The middle voice denotes a person is acting for himself, or is personally interested in someone's condition or welfare.[48] Certainly, the middle voice is signified in Heb. 2:3, by meaning and verb form. No one is likely to give religious testimony without caring if it is believed or hears it without deciding there and then if he believes it. The author of Hebrews secured the word of salvation for himself, or felt confirmation of the word of salvation. This is indeed a conversion story and not a hearing of testimony without assent to it. The author of Hebrews was converted by persons who had seen Jesus.

Was Apollos converted by those who had seen Jesus? No.

When he came to Ephesus he knew only the baptism of John - a pre-Christian state. He did not become a Christian until Priscilla and Aquila took him in hand and instructed him. The couple had lived in Rome. How could they have seen Jesus? Nor was the word accompanied by signs and wonders for Apollos, as for the author (see Heb. 2:4).

For Apollos, the conversion story doesn't check out. For this reason alone, he couldn't have written the Epistle to the Hebrews. Luther's guess was graced with a semblance of credibility, but credibility is not confirmation.

Apollos, whose path has crossed with that of Priscilla and Aquila is dismissed from the line-up. He is not the author, but has he had a fateful encounter with the author? Let's plan to resume this line of investigation.

Aristion - And His Entourage

Now we focus our attention upon Aristion, an unlikely suspect if ever we saw one. Aristion, or Ariston, is one of those minor suspects for whom there is no credible case. Indeed, there are far more credible grounds for dismissal. He represents a category of persons such as Silas, Epaphras, and Philip the deacon, whom Attridge. describes as shadowy figures not warranting serious consideration.[49]

Nonetheless John Chapman. concluded that the same person who wrote the last twelve chapters of Mark also wrote Hebrews, and that person was Aristion. He advanced this opinion in an article titled "Aristion, Author of the Epistle to the Hebrews."[50] A simple exercise in reasoning establishes the negative case against Aristion, and the lack of support for a positive case.

According to church historian Eusebius, Aristion was the informant of Bishop Papias of Hierapolis, concerning Jesus. Papias called Aristion "the Lord's disciple." As such, Aristion was an eye-witness to the ministry of Jesus, and thereby ineligible to have written the conversion story in Heb. 2:3. This is the negative case. Aristion was not of Paul's circle, did not have connections at Rome, from where Hebrews was circulated, and where the epistle was influenced by the Roman liturgy. There is no evidence that he was likely to have travelled with Timothy. There is no ancient testimony that he was the author of Hebrews, nor is there any reason why his name should have been lost had he been the author. There is simply no positive evidence linking him with Hebrews.

Now for Chapman's. argument. F. C. Coneybeare theorized that an Armenian manuscript dated 989, attributing Mark 16:9-20 to "the Presbyter Ariston" preserved a genuine tradition.[51] Chapman juxtaposed Mark 16:17-20 with Heb. 2:2-4, passages referring to signs and wonders. Then he compared Mark 16:17 with Heb. 11, claiming similitude of style and content. The passage in Mark recounts outward signs accompanying faith,[52] such as taking up serpents with impunity. The corresponding passage in Hebrews recounts the development of supernatural courage, daring, and fortitude. The identification of the author of one document as the author of the other is not so much a leap of faith as a leap of imagination.

Chapman. would have done better to juxtapose Mark 16:9-20 with the earlier section of Mark, Ch. 1:9-20. This is what John Burgon did to demonstrate the "essential parallelism" inherent in these portions of the gospel.[53] *In both pericopes*, he traces the proclamation from Heaven, the victory over Satan, the Pentecostal Gift, the preaching of repentance, the announcement of the Kingdom, and the Apostles' ministry, miraculously attested.

When Chapman claims for his hypothesis "a high degree of probability," he is really overstating his case.

In the line-up, between Aristion and Aquila and Priscilla, we see an indistinct figure. He is the hypothetical "unknown person," an unknown leader of the early church who allegedly is not mentioned in scripture. It is difficult to demonstrate that he shouldn't be there, since we don't know who he is, or even if he exists.

Reason informs us that such eloquence, articulating so high and exalted a faith, made the author eminent. As one of Paul's inner circle, this person is certainly named in scripture. Yet, there is the unsubstantial figure, like a wraith. He is not reasonable, he is not real, and he will not go away willingly but must be dispelled.

Many commentators cling to him, solemnly proclaiming that he is the author of Hebrews. The more evidence accrues to substantiate Harnack's theory, the more vivid our perception of a female author of scripture, the more emphatic the assurance, by some, that Mr. Nobody wrote Hebrews and we ought to discontinue the inquiry. We can be equally certain that our search is not in vain, that a prime suspect is in the line-up, and sheer weight of evidence will eventually reveal the author's identity.

Despite his lack of materiality, and the tenacity with which he stalks the line-up, Mr. Nobody or the hypothetical "unknown person," must meet the same criteria as anyone else. He must be of Paul's circle, not an eye-witness of Jesus, but the disciple of an apostle, with connections at Rome and a ministry to Hebrew Christians who reside in the city to which the letter was first sent. He must be expert in Greek, trained in rhetoric. There must be a cogent explanation for the loss of his name - one that will de-mystify the search process. If his name was lost because he wasn't mentioned in scripture, we still have to explain how so impressive an individual, close to Paul, escaped mention.

Once we decide the author of Hebrews was in fact named in scripture, we can make a list of New Testament personages and check them off one by one to see if they qualify for authorship. If disqualified for one reason or another, (for example: "not of Paul's circle" that person is crossed off the list. Next, compile positive evidence (for example: "was known as a teacher and leader"). If positive evidence is lacking or flimsy, the person should be dismissed as a finalist in favor of a more realistic alternative.

Always keep in mind, the author must be feminine in viewpoint, with a strong sense of identification with women. Which brings us to a suspect who *is* a woman.

NOTES TO CHAPTER V

1. Attridge., *op. cit.*, p. 2
2. Eusebius, *The History of the Church from Christ to Constantine*, transl. G. A. Williamson (Baltimore: Penguin Books, 1965), p. 254.
3. Westcott, p. xxxiv.
4. Except Heb. 10:30, quoting Deuteronomy 32:35.
5. Eusebius, p. 254.
6. William Leonard, *The Authorship of the Epistle to the Hebrews: Critical Problem and Use of the Old Testament* (Rome, Vatican: Polyglot Press, 1939).
7. Wikenhauser, p. 40.
8. Westcott, p. lxxv.
9. Eusebius, p. 149.
10. Clement's Letter to the Corinthian, *The Library of Christian Classics, Vol. I Early Christian Fathers*, transl. and ed. Cyril C. Richardson *et al.* (Philadelphia: The Westminster Press, 1953), p. 48-49.
11. *Ibid.*, p. 6
12. *Ibid.*, p. 43 (All italics are mine.)
13. *Ibid.*, p. 39
14. I Cor. 12 and Heb. 2:4.
15. Clement, chapter 44.
16. "Barnabae titulus ad Hebraeos." Westcott, p. xxviii.
17. Cameron, Ritschl, Weiss, Renan, Salmon, Vernon Bartlett, Ullman and Wieseler.
18. *Butler's Lives of the Saints*, Vol. 111. Complete edition, ed. Herbert Thurston and Donald Attwater (New York: P. J. Kennedy & Sons, n.d.), p. 522.
19. Alexander Roberts and James Donaldson, ed. *The Ante-Nicene Fathers. Vol. I: The Apostolic Fathers-Justin Martyr-Irenaeus.* (Grand Rapids: Wm. B. Eerdman's Publishing Co., 1950), p. 133.
20. *Butler's Lives of the Saints*, Vol. III, p. 524.

21. Codex Sinaiticus has "Epistle of Barnabas"; Dressel gives "Epistle of Barnabas the Apostle" from the Vatican manuscript of the Latin text. *Ante-Nicene Fathers*, Vol. I, p. 137.

22. Westcott, p. lxxx.

23. *Ibid.*, p. lxxv.

24. *Ante-Nicene Fathers*, Vol. I, p. 134.

25. *Ibid.*

26. Barnabas xvi: 8, 12, 13.

27. Heb. 3:16-19.

28. *The Jerusalem Bible, New Testament*, p. 265.

29. *Matthew Henry's Commentary on the Whole Bible, Vol. VI, Acts to Revelation.* (New York: Fleming H. Revell Co., n.d.), p. 88.

30. *Expositor's Greek Testament*, p. 222. See footnote 15.

31. Wikenhauser, p. 469 and *The Interpreter's Bible in Twelve Volumes*, Vol. XI, "The Epistle to the Hebrews" by C. Purdy and J. Harry Cotton, p. 590.

32. Eugenia Price, *God Speaks to Women Today*. (Grand Rapids: Zondervan Publishing Co., 1964), p. 180.

33. Butler, *op. cit.*, p. 524 and John Coulson, ed. *The Saints: A Concise Biographical Dictionary* (New York: Hawthorn Books, Inc., 1958), p. 62-63.

34. F. L. Cross, ed., *Oxford Dictionary of the Christian Church* (London: Oxford University Press, 1958), p. 132.

35. "How shall we escape if we neglect such a great salvation? It was declared at first by the Lord, *and it was attested to us by those who heard him*" (Italics mine)

36. *Outlines*, Bk. VIII. See Eusebius, *op. cit.*, p. 64.

37. Eusebius, p. 64.

38. Attridge., *op. cit.*, p. 3.

39. Leonard, *op. cit.*, p. 278.

40. J. Hering, Bleek, Th. Zahn, Appel, Rohr, Vogels and Spicq.

41. Clement 47:6. *Early Church Fathers*, Vol. I.

42. Hugh Montefiore, *A Commentary on the Epistle to the Hebrews.* (New York: Harper & Row, Publishers, 1964), p. 9.

43. Arthur S. Peake, *A Critical Introduction to the New Testament.* (New York: Charles Scribner's Sons, 1919), p. 80.

44. H. V. Morton, *In the Steps of St. Paul.* (New York: Dodd, Mead & Co., 1936), p. 353.

45. Montefiore, p. 19-28.

46. Wikenhauser, p. 308.

47. John Allegro, *The Dead Sea Scrolls.* (Baltimore: Penguin Books, Inc., 1956, p. 128 and 164. See also Millar Burrows, *The Dead Sea Scrolls* (New York: The Viking Press, 1955), 328-329, (New York: Gramercy Publishing Co., 1986)

48. W. E. Vine, *New Testament Greek Grammar* (Grand Rapids: Zondervan Publishing House, 1965), p. 128-129.

49. Attridge., p. 5.

50. John Chapman., "Aristion, Author of the Epistle to the Hebrews," *Revue Benedictine* 22 (1905)50-64.

51. *Oxford Dictionary of the Christian Church*, p.82.

52. Nairne, *op. cit.*, Notes, p. 39.

53. John W. Burgon, *The Last Twelve Verses of Mark.* (The Sovereign Grace Book Club, 1959), p. 263-264.

CHAPTER SIX

WE MEET THE AUTHOR

Apollos, who did not write Hebrews, will lead us to the author if we keep our eyes and ears open.

Self-assured and driven by a spiritual quest, he disembarked at Ephesus and headed for the synagogue. His goal: to give voice to messianic expectations, to inform and convince. A cultured and articulate orator, Apollos mesmerized the audience. Steeped in scripture, he won their respect. Not on the agenda: a man and woman in the audience sought him out and took him home. A strange day had dawned for their intellectual guest who, in a turnabout of roles, began to receive instruction.

That day, learned Apollos became the pupil of Priscilla and Aquila. Luke records the event, naming Priscilla before Aquila (Acts 18:26). From this we may infer that Priscilla was the primary teacher. With admirable insight, Chrysostom, Archbishop of Constantinople in the fourth century, named *Priscilla* the tutor: "...she (Priscilla) having taken Apollos, an eloquent man, et cetera, taught him the way of God and made him a perfect teacher..."[1]

We have already seen that Apollos, who heretofore "knew only the baptism of John," was, in effect, converted by Priscilla and Aquila. Harnack, in a study of women in the early church, avers: "...it was the woman who - as Chrysostom rightly infers ... - converted Apollos, the disciple of John the Baptist."[2]

Luke gives additional clues to the nature and content of Priscilla's teaching. We can be sure her teaching was intensive and comprehensive. The translation of Acts 18:26 in the NRSV, "they took him aside and explained the Way of God more accurately" is less telling than "they took him and expounded to him the way of God more accurately" (RSV) or "they took him home"...(NAB). The word translated "expounded" is ἐξέθεντο from ἐκτίθημι "to explain, set forth." The same word appears in Acts 28:23, where Paul *expounds* the Kingdom of God from scripture, lecturing all day.

Stop and think. If Apollos was "mighty in the scriptures" (Acts 18:24) so was Priscilla, his teacher. Harnack and others have observed that since Apollos was a cultured Greek, Priscilla herself was a person of culture as well as learning. Her role in teaching Apollos reveals her as one who is comparable to him in learning, spiritual insight, and experience in the mission field.

Since Apollos, as we have seen, knew only the baptism of John, he needed to be baptized as were other followers of John the Baptist (Acts 19:5). Luke does not "construct a baptism by Aquila" and no exegetes have suggested "he could be suppressing a baptism by Priscilla," according to Professor Antoinette Clark Wire[3] - implying, of course, that his mentors, Priscilla and Aquila, remain the likeliest ones to have baptized Apollos.

The time had come for Apollos to leave for Corinth. Corinth was unfamiliar territory for him, so he needed a letter of introduction. Again, who was most likely to provide such a letter? Let's think about this for a moment. Perhaps someone who knew that Apollos was qualified to preach the gospel? Perhaps someone who had been a church leader in Corinth and knew the people in that city? Priscilla, perhaps?

Not according to Acts 18:27, which relates noncommittally that "the brethren" in Ephesus composed the letter. Harnack thought that Priscilla was the actual writer,[4] and Donald Wayne Riddle says in an offhand way that when Apollos went to Corinth, Priscilla and Aquila "provided him with a letter urging that he be received there."[5] George A. Barton posits more than one letter, or several copies: "Aquila and Priscilla encouraged him and gave him letters of introduction."[6]

There is more to observe about the fateful meeting of Apollos with Priscilla and Aquila. As might be expected, Apollos was an apt student. Once he arrived in Corinth he began to preach that Jesus was the Messiah foretold in scripture. Bible in hand, he powerfully confuted the opposition. If Apollos could prove from scripture that Jesus was the Messiah, it was only because Priscilla had previously instructed him on this theme. Only following her instruction did he become an effective spokesman for the Christian faith, whose specialty was proving Jesus to be the Messiah.

The subject of Apollos' preaching is the subject Priscilla taught him, and that subject is identical with the main theme of the Epistle to the Hebrews.

A striking coincidence. Or is it more than coincidence?

If we hypothesize that Priscilla wrote the Epistle to the Hebrews, we have an hypothesis that explains this particular coincidence, as "a true theory explains *all* coincidences."

All told, there are six references to Priscilla and her husband in the Bible.[7] Four times her name is before Aquila's, a hint of Priscilla's pre-eminence.[8] Another possible reason for naming the woman first, contrary to custom, must be considered. If she were of higher birth than her husband, according to E. H. Plumptre and others, in the "common formula of social usage..., her name would naturally take precedence."[9]

Aquila was a Christian evangelist in his own right, caught up in the challenge and excitement of their life. Praise to God resounded in their home as Christians sang and prayed. Aquila and his wife were co-leaders of a house-church in Rome. Claudius' edict banishing Jews from Rome[10] led them to Corinth where a close friendship with Paul ensued.

It is generally assumed that Paul met Priscilla and Aquila by happenstance, or as a result of their common occupation. However, Verna J. Dozier and James R. Adams, co-authors of *Sisters and Brothers*, have a different idea:

> ...Paul found Aquila and Priscilla in Corinth, presumably because *he was looking for them* (italics mine).[11]

The word translated "found" in Luke and Acts has two shades of meaning. In Acts 11:26 and Luke 11:24, for example, it means to find after searching. In Luke 4:17 and Acts 17:23 it means to find accidentally. Lexicons cite "to find after searching" as more common, but context must be weighed.

Which meaning applies to Acts 18:2?

In Acts 18:2,3 we then read that Paul "went to see them" and because they were of the same trade, stayed with them. Did Paul "go to see them" after an initial, accidental encounter, or did he first find out where they lived, and then go to see them? If Paul were, in fact, looking for Priscilla and Aquila before he met them, this underscores their importance in the church at Rome.

In either case, home in Corinth was "church headquarters" for Paul had moved in with them (Acts 18:3). Paul came to rely on their able dedication to Christ. When he sailed for Syria, he took Priscilla and Aquila with him (Acts 18:18).

The same arrangement that served the trio in Corinth, with Paul residing under the same roof, may have continued in Ephesus. Edmundson surmises: "Probably their house was as before the Apostle's home", citing manuscript evidence.[12]

In I Cor. 16:19, written from Ephesus, Paul sends greetings from Aquila and Prisca, and the church in their house, adding, in various manuscripts "παρ οἷς καὶ ζενίζομαι *(with whom also I am a guest).*"[13]

"With whom also I am a guest": this significant phrase occurs in a group of manuscripts known as D, F, lat, goth, Bede., indicative of the tradition in the Western Church that Paul lived with the pair at Ephesus.[14]

A picture emerges of a couple who take on major leadership responsibilities. Add to the sketch their hospitality that is sharply outlined in the New Testament. Except for the well-to-do, first century homes and apartments were small. Only wealthier Christians with spacious homes could provide a room large enough for worshipers.

Nor were gatherings a once-weekly convocation. At first, Christians met daily for prayer. In the hospitality of Priscilla and Aquila, we glimpse their relative affluence.

Paul boarded with them in Corinth, grateful for a place to live and work (Acts 18:3). There had been times when he knew want, even to the point of not having enough to eat:

> *I know how to be abased, and I know how to abound; in any and all circumstances I have learned the secret of facing plenty and hunger, abundance and want (Phil. 4:12).*

Apparently, tentmaking was not always profitable. And in his travels Paul received no financial aid from his wealthy family.

By contrast, Paul's two friends could afford a place to live, roomy enough for a live-in guest as well as for meetings and worship. Their financial superiority to Paul can be explained in this way: Priscilla was wealthy. Industrious, she worked to keep busy and to set a good example, while Aquila supported himself and his wife by his trade.

If Priscilla were simply a leader of the church, we could put it down to intelligence and religious zeal. But if she wrote the Epistle to the Hebrews, we have to find out how she acquired a knowledge of classical literature and Old Testament scripture, so marked in the Epistle. If she came from a wealthy family, her education in literature and philosophy is accounted for.

This takes us to the core of our study. Neither Paul, Clement, Barnabas, nor Apollos wrote Hebrews, but Apollos has led us to a prime suspect. Let's feed some facts about Priscilla into the computer and see if it can identify her as the author.

Truth Dug Out of the Earth

The truth about Priscilla and her family was literally unearthed, for it comes out of the underground burial places of Rome. Study of Roman catacombs has established two salient facts:

1. She knew Peter in Rome. This is germane to our study, for it ties in with the mode of conversion of Priscilla and Aquila.
2. She was of an illustrious Roman family, which confirms her scholarly and cultural qualifications.

The Conversion Story Checks Out for Priscilla

We have a good clue to the way Priscilla and Aquila were converted to Christianity. They lived in Rome. Rome first heard the gospel from Jewish Christians who fled Palestine and Syria.[15] Geographically, these Jewish Christians had every chance to be eyewitnesses to the ministry of Jesus. Peter arrived in 42-43 A.D.

The first Christian converts in the city came from its Jewish population,[16] and others who attended the synagogue. Converts like Priscilla, wife of Aquila, a Jew, who could say that persons who heard Jesus spoke the word of salvation to them (Heb. 2:3).

Undeniably, Priscilla was converted in Rome, for upon her arrival in Corinth she was already a church leader. Nor would Paul, a Christian missionary, be likely to find lodgings with her and Aquila if they were a Jewish couple expelled from Rome because of conflict with Christians.[17]

Evidence connects her with a famous Roman family, and in Rome she resided. Aquila, born in Pontus near the Black Sea in Asia Minor, is thought to be a freed slave. He lived in Rome long enough to win his freedom and a wife. (Her family may have been his clients.) There is no evidence placing them outside Rome during Peter's sojourn.

Re LXXVIIII

IMP. CAES. M. AVR. SEVERO ALEXANDRO

COS IDIB APRILIBVS

CONCILIVM CONVENTVS CLVNIENS

G. MARIVM PVDENTEM CORNELIA

NVM LEG LEG C V PATRONVM

SIBI LIBERIS POSTERISQVE SVIS

COOPTAVIT OB MVLTA ET EGREGIA

EIVS IN SINGVLOS VNIVERSOS

MERITA PER LEGATVM

VAL MARCELLVM

CLVNIENSEM

In tabula quae inventa apud S. Priscam nunc in Biblio=
theca Vaticana

Orelli, 956.

EXHIBIT A: Notice to Pope Pius VI of discovery of a bronze plaque in the domicile of Priscilla.

Courtesy, Bibliothèque Nationale de France.

Epitaph of a "Priscilla" and her brother M. Acilius.
Hypogaeum, Priscilla Catacomb

Priscilla was a common name in the Acilian family.

Courtesy, Benedictine Sisters

Anchor, Cross and Fish, Priscilla Catacomb

The anchor is prevalent in the Priscilla Catacomb (Heb. 6:19)

Courtesy, Benedictine Sisters

In fact, if Priscilla wrote Heb. 2:3, she was assuredly thinking of Peter - a surpassing example of a man who heard the news of salvation from Jesus.

Priscilla Meets Peter

Arthur S. Barnes thinks Peter accompanied Priscilla and Aquila when Claudius banished Jews from Rome.[18] He may be right. Peter had ardent followers in Corinth. His presence there is a "must" to explain the faction that grew around him (I Cor. 1:12; 3:21b,22). Bishop Dionysius, in 170 A.D., writes of Peter and Paul who "sowed in our Corinth and taught us jointly."[19] Then Peter, like Paul, was in Corinth with Priscilla and Aquila.

Priscilla and Aquila knew Peter before they fled to Corinth. We turn our attention to Rome, where they met.

Closely following the first Christian immigrants, Peter came to Rome in 42 or 43 A.D., according to Jerome.[20] Eusebius dates his first visit to Rome in the reign of Claudius (41-54 A.D.).[21] All first century reporters say that Peter was the first apostle to preach in Rome.[22] One of Peter's converts was Pudens, a Roman senator. Very early tradition equates him with the Pudens named by Paul in II Tim. 4:21. By the same tradition, he opened his home to both Peter and Paul.[23] In this home on the Aventine, Peter is said to have offered the bread and wine of the Communion meal.[24]

So Peter stayed or visited in the home of Pudens, where he led religious services. How do we connect Priscilla with Pudens, and thus with Peter? Priscilla and Pudens were members of the same family. This claim deserves and will receive careful authentication.

Before we go ahead with our argument, I want to talk about "Tradition," a key word. "Tradition" is a flashing yellow word, signalling us to proceed with caution. This we will do. If we find a *late* tradition, far removed from apostolic times, we may be dealing with a legend. "Legend" is a red word that will bring us to a dead stop. If, on the other hand, our tradition is *early*, and if we can trace it back to a reliable source, then we can match it with other facts to see if it fits.

For instance, an early tradition held that Pudens' house was under the Church of St. Pudenziani (or Pudentia), named for his daughter. In 1870 some men were digging under this church. They broke into a spacious brick building - the house of Pudens. When their spades struck brick they hit what we are justified to call solid evidence.

In the eighteenth century a series of archeological finds began, having to do with Priscilla. One of these discoveries evinces that Priscilla's house was on Pudens' estate. First I will describe the discoveries. Then we will draw some obvious conclusions.

The ancient Church of St. Prisca, on the Aventine, was built over the house of Priscilla and Aquila, according to venerable tradition - traceable, perhaps, to apostolic times. Until the fourteenth century, an inscription declaring its apostolic origin adorned the architrave. Catacombs scholars De Rossi and Marucchi found remarkable corroborative evidence.

According to them, two important discoveries had been made in the eighteenth century. The narrative reads like a mystery story. First there was digging in the garden near the church, leading to the excavation of an ancient Christian oratory. A few years later there was digging closer to the church structure, leading to the excavation of an ancient Roman house. This is how Tuker and Malleson tell the story:

> ...remains of an ancient Roman house were excavated close to the basilica, and in it was found an inscription upon bronze, now in the Vatican Library, referring to the owner of the house *Cornelianus Pudenti*, senator of Rome in the year 222. Unfortunately these interesting ruins have been destroyed, but the records left of their discovery and the circumstance that the dwelling of Cornelius of the family of Pudens was upon this spot, are sufficient to show the

> close relation between the *domus Priscae* on the Aventine and the *domus Pudentianae* on the Esquiline, and present a valuable confirmation of the tradition that this is the "*ecclesia domestica*" of Priscilla.[25]

H. V. Morton, recounting his visit to the Church of St. Priscilla, and citing the apostolic tradition that it was built over the house of Aquila and Priscilla, has this to say:

> ...there is...a curious mystery connected with this church which deserves the attention of archaeologists. In the year 1776 a subterranean oratory was discovered near the Church of St. Prisca. The walls were decorated with fourth-century frescoes. Without even drawing a plan or copying the frescoes, the discoverers apparently walled up the oratory again. There is little doubt that this was the original site of the house of Aquila and Priscilla.
>
> The only notice of this extraordinary discovery is written on a scrap of paper preserved in the Bibliothèque Nationale in Paris, signed by a man named Carrara and addressed to the Treasurer of Pope Pius VI. So far as I know, no attempt has been made since that time to uncover the oratory.[26]

More about the oratory and its ancient frescoes:

> ...This house (of Priscilla and Aquila) became one of the first oratories where Christian prayer, in Rome, rose to God. Paul, upon his stay in Rome, had every reason to go there and speak to the faithful, and this remembrance was worthy of a consecration never more forgotten, hence a sanctuary was erected on this site once the peace afforded the Church in the 4th century made it possible to commemorate long-ago yet steadfast traditions. ...Other findings attest to the fact that the memory of the apostles was attached to the corner of the hill where Saint Priscilla stands. Under Pius VI, an

> ancient oratory was uncovered there, decorated with paintings dating approximately to the 4th century, in which images of the apostles remained. It is there,..that, according to Bianchini, in his commentaries in the *Liber pontificalis*, an engraved glass from the 4th or 5th century, decorated with recessed effigies depicting the apostles, was uncovered, on which three names could still be made out: *Petrus, Andreas, Philippus.* De Rossi indicated another analogous glass unearthed in his time in the vineyard of the Roman school (*College*) near Saint Priscilla: "Is it not curious, it is said, to encounter such undying testimony to the apostles in this place which is reputed to have been honored by the presence of Peter and Paul, residing with Aquila and Priscilla? Can one not see in the persistent tenacity of these remembrances a confirmation of the popular information, and rely thereon to locate in this place the home of these two important people?"[27]

The reference to Paul residing with Aquila and Priscilla is interesting; we have already mentioned the ancient tradition that Pudens opened his home to both Peter and Paul. Undoubtedly Paul enjoyed the hospitality of Priscilla's relatives sometime during his stay in Rome.

We find in another codex, Vat. lat. 1193, 46rb, a collection of three sermons on Aquila and Priscilla, by Peter the Deacon of the historic Benedictine Abbey of Monte Cassino. Monte Cassino, rebuilt after World War II, is the principal monastery of the Benedictine Order.[28] Peter the Deacon (1075-1139), writing in Latin, conveyed this information:

> "the apostolic authority consecrated the house of the blessed Aquilo and Prisca in honour of the catholic church and gave it the name of the Holy and Undivided (or, indivisible). In the church the apostolic authority ordered a baptistery with a perpetual fountain to be built."[29]

I am indebted to Leonard E. Boyle, of Bibliotheca Apostolica Vaticana, for his translation. Boyle presumes that the "apostolic authority" refers to Peter and Paul.

Peter the Deacon, though writing in the twelfth century, referred to ancient and prevalent tradition. This document, with its reference to a baptistery, testifies to a spacious, important place of worship in the house of Priscilla and Aquila. Since church buildings were not constructed until the fourth century, reference to a baptistery in a private home in apostolic times is all the more striking.

Exhibit A - A Bronze Tablet in an Ancient Roman House

H. V. Morton referred to a "scrap of paper" serving notice to Pope Pius VI of the discovery of an ancient oratory on the site of Priscilla and Aquila's domicile. This notice, a Vatican codex unceremoniously printed in block letters on a single page,[30] documents the above-mentioned bronze plaque, found at the site. The tablet, dated 224 A.D., commemorates an honor given to a senator, Caius Marius Pudens Cornelianus. (A Spanish city conferred citizenship upon him.)[31]

So a bronze tablet, inscribed with the name of Pudens Cornelianus, was unearthed under the ancient Church of St. Prisca on the Aventine, named for Aquila's wife.[32] As the church was built over the residence of Priscilla and Aquila,[33] the tablet was, in effect, discovered in their house. Meaning, of course, they lived on property belonging to the Cornelian family.[34] Understandably, such inscriptions were placed where the man lived who was being honored - or where his descendants lived.

Since she and her husband lived on the estate of Pudens' family, they were either servants or members of the family. If they were servants, why was the bronze tablet placed in their home? Why wasn't it placed in Pudens' home, under the Church of St. Pudentia, or in the building under the Church of St. Prassedis? The latter churches, both on Pudens' estate, are named for his two daughters.[35] Apparently, Priscilla and Aquila were members of the family. The bronze tablet is Exhibit A in the case for Priscilla being a relative of Pudens - and a high-born Roman woman.

One other point: If Priscilla lived on the estate of Pudens' family, how could she easily avoid meeting Peter, Pudens' guest? His presence, virtually at her doorstep, signifies that Priscilla knew Peter.

Exhibit B - Via Salaria 430

Exhibit B is nothing less than a vast underground City of the Dead - the Cemetery of Priscilla on the Via Salaria. In these catacombs we will find dramatic proof that Peter was closely associated with Pudens (and Priscilla). Here we will meet the rest of Priscilla's family.

The Cemetery of Priscilla, rediscovered in the first half of the nineteenth century, was described by Baronius.[36] Very much to the point, it is on - or rather, under - Pudens' estate. It was named for his mother, not for Aquila's wife.[37]

The Priscilla Cemetery originated in the first century. Testifying to its antiquity are crypts dating from the first and second centuries. Type and phraseology of inscriptions, and frequent use of Greek in the epitaphs all point to a very ancient date.[38] As Edmundson states: "The oldest parts of the Catacomb of Priscilla are regarded by De Rossi, Marucchi, Lanciani and the best authorities as dating from the middle of the first century. The most ancient inscriptions are in red and many in the Greek language."[39]

Bettenson, too, records several inscriptions from the first century. [40]

Edmundson comments on "the appearance of the name of Peter both in Greek and Latin, among the inscriptions of the most ancient Christian cemeteries, *especially in the first-century catacomb of Priscilla*" (italics mine). He continues: "The appearance of this unusual name on these early Christian tombs can most easily be explained by the supposition that either those who bore it or their parents had been baptised by Peter."[41]

Peter Baptized in the Cemetery of Priscilla

If Peter preached, taught and baptized in the Catacombs of Priscilla, it means that he carried out his work on Pudens' property, right by Priscilla's home.

References to the *Coemeterium ad Nymphas beati Petri ubi baptizaverat* or "Cemetery of the fountains where Peter baptized"[42] can be traced back to the fifth century.[43] At one time the scene of Peter's ministry was thought to be the Coemeterium Ostrianum.[44] With the discovery of the Cemetery of Priscilla we now know otherwise. Explorers found a big reservoir on the first of its two stories, and smaller ones in various corridors.[45] With startling aptness the Priscilla Catacomb fits the description *ad Nymphas* (of fountains) better than any other.

In a dramatic demonstration, Marucchi showed scholars pools filled with water in the crypts of the Catacomb. Imagine! Perhaps the very place where Peter preached and where he baptized his first converts![46] Did he baptize Priscilla and Aquila? Deductive reasoning points like an arrow in that direction.

We have talked about Peter and Priscilla, and how we know they were Christian associates for many years. Two facts emerge from their friendship. First, to repeat: Priscilla could have written the conversion story in Heb. 2:3, mindful of Peter who heard the Lord Jesus. Of utmost importance is the second point: the Jewish philosopher-theologian Philo of Alexandria, whose writings are echoed in the Epistle to the Hebrews, had long conversations with Peter in Rome. Priscilla, being on the scene, was in on the discussions, we can be sure. Here is the story:

Philo went to Rome in 40 A.D. to defend the Jews of Alexandria accused by the Greeks of failing to honor Caesar. Emperor Gaius curtly ordered him out, refusing to hear his appeal.[47] Bear in mind, in the reign of Gaius (37-41 A.D.) Philo was renowned as a scholar, even among Pagans. Philo, more than a little piqued, immortalized Gaius' misdeeds in a work called "Virtue" - a satirical title.

When Claudius became Emperor, Philo read the entire essay to the Roman Senate. By then, he was so acclaimed that his writings were in Roman libraries.[48] During this second visit Philo is reported to have held conversations with Peter. Eusebius even says that Philo came to Rome to meet Peter.[49]

You can understand the pertinence of Philo's stay in Rome and the fact that his writings were known and honored there. Many scholars, citing the influence of Philo in the Epistle to the Hebrews, decided that like Philo, the author lived in Alexandria. This is one reason why Apollos, an Alexandrian, was a popular candidate. But now we see that Priscilla, living in Rome, had a chance to read Philo's works, to talk with him and to use some of his ideas.

This is rather an important point because parallels with Philo are pervasive in Hebrews. Johannes B. Capzov originated an area of research when, in 1750, he found parallels from Philo for almost every verse of the epistle.[50] One salient example is the Platonic idea, advanced in Philo, that the world is shadow or sketch of a heavenly model. Throughout chapters eight and nine in Hebrews, the author distinguishes between the real sanctuary in heaven and the earthly sanctuary, a shadowy symbol. Other examples can be given.

Nonetheless, Priscilla was Peter's disciple - not Philo's! As a Christian evangelist and teacher, she had to be rooted in Biblical history and doctrine.

Nowhere in Hebrews do we find Philo's penchant for allegory. Platonic concepts, borrowed from Philo, subserve the development of Christian teaching. By contrasting the heavenly and earthly sanctuary, the author utilizes a Platonic idea, in Philo, to illustrate a point. As high priest in the heavenly sanctuary, Jesus is mediator of a new covenant - in fulfillment of the old covenant, represented by an earthly tabernacle (Heb. 9:15).

Philo's Platonism is only a launching pad for the author's teaching:

> For Christ has entered, not into a sanctuary made with hands, a copy of the true one, but into Heaven itself, now to appear in the presence of God in our behalf (Heb. 9:24 RSV).

To recapitulate, as a resident of Rome, associated with Peter, likely acquainted with Philo personally, Priscilla could well have written Hebrews with its Philonic parallels subserving Christian teaching.

Exhibit C - A Remarkable Discovery in the Priscilla Cemetery

Back to the catacombs on the trail of Priscilla's family. Just as her house relates her to Pudens, so does her burial place. The tombs of Priscilla and Aquila are in the Priscilla Catacombs, along with the tombs of Senator Pudens[51] of the Cornelian family and his two daughters.[52] Tuker and Malleson state: "The Martyrologies, the Acta, the Itineraries, all state that that they were buried here. Another confirmation of Priscilla's relation to the mother of Pudens."[53]

I am indebted to Joan Morris, author, linguist and art historian, who wrote to me in 1972 about her visit to the Catacomb of Priscilla. She mentioned Marucchi's list of people buried there, a list including "Prudentia and Praxedis, the daughters of Pudens, who were members of the Acili Glabriones family, and Aquila and Priscilla of the same family."[54]

Certain others were removed from the crypts in the fourth century, but the bodies of Pudens and his daughters, and Aquila and Priscilla were left undisturbed "until the time of Leo IV in the middle of the ninth century."[55] Although relics of these and other notable people were removed in the ninth century, their burial in the Priscilla Catacomb is mentioned in the following ancient documents:

Calendario Filocaliano
Gli'Itinerari
Liber Pontificalis
The Catalogue of Manza.[56]

In 1988, I had an opportunity to visit the Priscilla Catacomb. Sister Maria Francesca of the Benedictine Sisters, who are caretakers of the Catacomb, and reside in "The House of Priscilla," took me on a special tour. I saw the hypogaeum, which, she explained, dates from the first century. She told me that

Priscilla and Aquila had certainly been buried in the catacomb, although there was no identifiable tomb now marking the exact location.

Edmundson relates that a "well-authenticated tradition" places the tombs of Aquila and Prisca near an inscription mentioning Tertius, who may possibly have been Paul's amanuensis. Of great concern to us, this inscription is near the mausoleum of a noble Roman family.[57]

The year 1887 gave the world a find of vital import in its quest for the author of Hebrews. I call it *Exhibit C.*

The crypt of the noted family, the Acilii Glabriones, was discovered in the Priscilla Catacomb.[58] Moreover, their crypt is in the oldest part of the cemetery,[59] so they must be the family who originated the burial place. And the entrance to these catacombs is underneath the elegant residence of the Acilii family.[60]

This proves that the Cornelian family, of which Pudens was a member, and the Acilius families had a common burial place.[61] It also proves that they had property in common. After all, Pudens owned the cemetery built on his property. The Acilii family, wealthy and distinguised, would scarcely choose a borrowed tomb for themselves. Pudens belonged to the eminent house of the Acilii Glabriones, as De Rossi proposed.[62] His colleagues, leading Italian scholars, emphatically agree.[63] If Priscilla is related to Pudens, she is related to the Acilii Glabriones.

What's in a Name?

Did you notice a certain "coincidence"? Priscilla bears the same name as Pudens' mother, for whom the cemetery was named.[64] First names recurred in specific families in stereotyped fashion,[65] and Priscilla was a common first name in the Glabriones family.[66] Some examples can be cited:

First century: Pudens' mother, *Priscilla*

A Manius Acilius and his sister Priscilla are named on an inscription[67] in the hypogaeum.[68] (In my visit to the catacomb, I was interested to see a marble slab with the name "PRISCILLA" inscribed under "M ACILIUS").

Since the hypogaeum is the oldest part of the cemetery, we can take the inscription to be first century.

Second century: Several, including Arria Lucii filia Plaria Vera Priscilla, or "Arria Priscilla" - wife of the consul of 152 A.D., Manius Acilus Glabrio Cornelius Severus. He also had a daughter, *Priscilla.*[69]

Note that Aquila's wife lived on their property, and weigh the recurrence of the name Priscilla in the Glabriones family. There are three possibilities:

(1) She could be a servant (i.e., a slave or a freed woman) of the Cornelian or Acilian family, her name being mere coincidence.

(2) She could be a servant who assumed the name Priscilla for some reason.

(3) She could be a member of the family.

Some scholars think Aquila and Priscilla were both freed slaves, but Ramsay and others say she was a member of the family.[70] Many scholars still ignore discoveries in the Catacomb, and the entire question.

Let's check out the alternatives.

(1) Obviously, neither Aquila nor his wife had slave status. They were free to travel. Aquila may have been an ex-slave, but not Priscilla:

- Slaves were a foreign element, seized in other parts of the Empire and taken to Rome. Priscilla, who has a Roman name, was born in Rome, so far as we know.
- The bronze tablet honoring Pudens (Exhibit A) would not be placed in a servant's quarters in preference to the home of a relative.

- Whenever possible, house-churches were in the spacious homes of the affluent. Christians met often for prayer. I question if servants had time (and permission) to lead frequent services.

(2) Did Priscilla adopt her name? True, it was the custom for a freed slave to adopt the family name of the one who granted his freedom.[71] First names were no part of this custom. We have no reason to assume Priscilla once had a different name.

E. H. Plumptre contended:

> Her name, Priscilla, or, as it meets us in the better MSS. of 2 Tim. iv. 19, and Rom. xvi. 3, Prisca, was that of one of the most illustrious families of Rome. In the long list of those who bore it in its masculine form, Priscus (as we find them, *e.g.*, in Dr. Smith's "Dictionary of Classical Biography"), we meet with every variety of official rank: consuls, legates, praetors, quaestors, knights. *If we found the feminine name in any chapter of Tacitus or Suetonius, the natural inference would be that she was related by birth or adoption to some member of the gens (the house or clan) of these Prisci. There is no instance that I know of, of its being borne by a woman of Jewish origin.*[72] (Italics mine)

(3) Priscilla's learning and self-confidence support the theory of Sir William Ramsay. She was a Roman woman, born to an aristocratic family. Plumptre and other suggest that Paul's naming of Priscilla first, before Aquila, on some occasions, was a consequence of her higher social status.[73] Another inference drawn is that the house in Rome was her property.[74]

You may want to pose this question: could we have known from inscriptions on their tombs if Priscilla and Aquila were servants or relatives of the Acilian family? The answer is no.

Unlike their pagan neighbors, Christians inscribed only first names on tombs, with few exceptions.[75] Leaving us to track down Priscilla's family name, even if her tomb were located. The type and location of the tombs tell us no more. Spence-Jones explains that just as slaves were given equality in the life of the church, they were given equality with their owners in the "hospitality accorded them in death."[76] Slaves and freedmen were buried in corridors around the family crypt.[77] Hertling notes that many Acilians were buried in corridors around the family crypt, in the Cemetery of Priscilla.[78] From this, we deduce slaves, freedmen and their masters were not interred in segregated places.

Were the Glabriones a Christian family? Many were, though not all. Acilius Glabrio, consul in 91 A.D., was martyred by Domitian along with other Christians.[79] And in their crypt, Christian symbols are carved on sarcophagi bearing the family name.[80] Then we can add this fact about Priscilla: her family is known to have other Christian members besides Pudens and his daughters.

More About Priscilla's Family

The Acilian Glabriones were a prestigious family. Knowing the extent and nature of their eminence, we can better see how Priscilla attained to literary heights.

Pudens was a senator. If De Rossi is right, he may have been a consul.[81] Historians Suetonius and Dion Cassius record that Acilius Glabrio, head of the family, was consul in 91 A.D.[82] Nor was he alone in this exalted office. Nine members of the Manius Acilius Glabrio were consuls. Setting the precedent was Acilius Glabrio in 191 B.C.[83] Look at the genealogical chart on page 115. Please notice that a member of Priscilla's family was consul in 54 A.D., the year Nero succeeded Claudius. I will refer to this again.

What did it mean to be a consul? The next step up was Emperor. They may be likened to the American president. Wielding enormous political power in the republic (250-81 B.C.), they presided over the Senate. In time of war, the consul was commander in chief.[84] Even under the Empire, two consuls were elected each year, their office being one of high honor.[85] Granted, their powers were abridged.

But the title "consul", bestowed by the emperor, was "the greatest honor in the world" as late as the sixth century A.D.[86]

Consuls were derived from the aristocracy.[87] Others could not afford the job, for they were unpaid. They had to organize athletic games with all their pageantry. For this, and other expenses incurred by their office, they were not wholly reimbursed.[88]

A daughter of the nobility, Priscilla had a fine education. In the time of the Caesars, girls were often taught in non-segregated classes with boys, and went on to become intellectual equals of educated men.[89] In a wealthy family, she was sure to study Greek and Roman literature, and philosophy. Since she preached the gospel (as Tertullian records), she was capable in rhetoric. The ancient world valued oratory. Those who took part in it were expected to excel. We can see how and why she was trained for this role. Her skill is evident in Hebrews, a letter most impressive when read aloud.

In fact, Priscilla carried on a family tradition. Cicero reports that Manius Acilius Glabrio, consul in 95 B.C., was trained expertly in oratory by his maternal grandfather. Another forebear of Priscilla, M'. Acilius Glabrio, undoubtedly trained for the task, pleaded on behalf of one M. Aemilius Scaurus at Scaurus' trial in 54 B.C.[90]

It is also clear why she had leisure to pursue her religious interests. Upper-class Roman women, with money and slaves, could do pretty much as they pleased. Gifted with intellect and fluency, Priscilla spoke for her Savior. Infused with the same eloquence and logic, the letter to the Hebrews still edifies the church. Eugenia Price sums it up: "Priscilla was a *scholar*."[91]

Elsie Culver tags Priscilla "sophisticated."[92] Her self-confidence (an allied trait) was boundless and expressed in many ways: leading churches; traveling; working at a trade with her husband; mentoring the renowned Apollos. All this fits in with her family background.

We have already endorsed the premise: The author of Hebrews was "famous" - a person known to the early church, and no hypothetical obscure person can be seriously considered. Why? To review the reasons: A companion of Timothy, the author was of Paul's circle. Readers, urged to take hold of God's promises, were addressed by someone in a position of spiritual leadership. That someone had lived and taught among them for years. Now, the readers were in several congregations, for it was written: "Remember your leaders..." (Heb. 13:7). A teacher (or preacher)-at-large, over and above the leadership of a single house-church, of towering stature intellectually, culturally, and spiritually, our writer had wide influence.

Priscilla matches this description. Her fame is incontestable. Her name is carved on many Roman monuments including the Church of St. Prisca. Early Christian writers heaped praise upon her, extolling her courage, ability and holiness. A legend grew around her in the tenth century "Acts of St. Prisca."[93]

I would rather draw inferences from the Bible than any other source, and scripture is very clear on this point. Priscilla was known in several cities. From Ephesus, Paul conveyed "hearty greetings" from Aquila and Priscilla to the church of Corinth. Corinth remembered the woman who had been their inspired teacher, setting the tenor of their faith for eighteen months. She and her husband commanded the attention of *all* the churches in a dramatic way when Paul recorded his gratitude in these words:

> Greet Prisca and Aquila, my fellow workers in Christ Jesus, who risked their necks for my life, to whom not only I but also all the churches of the *Gentiles give thanks*; greet also the church in their house (Rom. 16:3,4). (Italics mine.)

Culver thinks Priscilla was known for an additional reason; it was she who copied and sent some of Paul's letters to the churches. Priscilla may have been Paul's "secretary," as Culver proposes. Her fame, however, was not derivative, and grew as the early church wonderingly watched her in action - teaching and preaching;

risking her life to rescue Paul; matching wits with Apollos, a leading theologian of her time, and bringing him into the Christian fold.

Culver has set forth a most intriguing hypothesis, which I am not prepared to defend, but cannot resist stating. In brief, the combination of Paul's unpolished style and Priscilla's literary skill was too much temptation for Priscilla. She "improved" the letters, not knowing what we know today - they were to become Holy Scripture. Priscilla's editing gave Paul's writing the occasional style and polish that have baffled New Testament critics.

According to Culver's theory, three letters are said to have been improved upon: Philippians, Philemon and Colossians. Paul wrote them in Ephesus in 52-55 A.D. Most scholars think they were revised at Rome in 59-61 A.D.[94] At that time, Culver says, Priscilla and Aquila were in Rome "on leave" from Ephesus. So Priscilla could have been the editor.

Culver adds that several copies of Romans (penned at Corinth in 55 A.D.) were found in Ephesus and other cities. Priscilla, who was in Ephesus for several years, acted as secretary circulating Romans to various cities. And *editing*.

Culver may be right. Priscilla and Aquila may have gone to Rome in 59 A.D. Perhaps they wanted to visit Priscilla's family. On the other hand, she is wrong to cite Rom. 16:3,4 as proof. Paul *did* greet the couple in Rom. 16:3,4. But part of the sixteenth chapter (vs. 1-20) is missing from certain very old manuscripts. For this and other reasons, many scholars think Rom. 16:1-20 was appended to a copy destined for Ephesus.[95] This does not confute Culver's theory that Priscilla was in Rome about 59 A.D., a viable possibility. But I do not grant Priscilla was there in 55 A.D. when Paul wrote the epistle, staying four or five years before going back to Ephesus. First, because a strong case can be made for the theory of Schulz and Renan that Rom. 16:1-20 was sent to Ephesus only.[96] Second, because we cannot place Priscilla and Aquila in Rome in 59 A.D. with any certainty.

We can only say that if some of Paul's letters were edited, it is possible Priscilla was the editor.

Where do we go from here?

It is beginning to make sense - good sense - to claim with Harnack and others that Priscilla is the author of the Epistle to the Hebrews. A few questions remain to be stated and answered.

Whoever wrote Hebrews knew more than literature and philosophy. That person had a solid grasp of Old Testament scripture. If Priscilla is the author we must explain how she came to a mastery of the Old Testament. We must decide if the author, apparently Jewish, was of necessity Jewish by birth as well as by faith. Then we want to know about Aquila. What was his social status? Is it reasonable to think of him being married to Priscilla, an intellectual aristocrat?

When these questions have been answered, I will proceed to show that Hebrews was addressed to the Jewish Christians of Ephesus, where Priscilla and Aquila had a long-standing ministry. Then I will offer an explanation for their temporary absence from Ephesus and how the letter to the Hebrews came to be written from Rome.

Priscilla Meets the Prophets

First century Judaism was a missionary faith. Many Gentile women rallied to its one God and high moral standards. Ramsay believes Priscilla was one of these proselytes.[97] The influence of Aquila, who was a Jew, and worked for Pudens, Priscilla's relative,[98] should also be taken into account.

When Priscilla cast her lot with the Jews of Rome, she became part of a sizeable community. Jews were numerous in Rome, as their catacombs testify.[99] Expelled by Claudius' edict, many returned after he died in 54 A.D. Soon they numbered about 25,000.[100] Their population is estimated between 30,000 and 50,000 in the reign of Nero (64-68 A.D.).[101] All in all, they had about thirteen synagogues.[102]

The very first Christian converts in Rome came from the synagogues.[103] A sign that the left wing branch of Judaism was represented in Rome. These Jews, known as Essenes, were related to - if not the same as - Qumran sectarians by the Dead Sea. Everywhere, they were among the first to accept the new faith. Jewish Christian migrants from Palestine and Syria had in their ranks many former Essenes.

A dialogue with Essene doctrine permeates the Epistle to the Hebrews. In Rome, Priscilla learned about the Jewish faith and this particular offshoot of it.

Scholarly and determined, Priscilla set out to study Hebrew scripture. Not knowing the Hebrew text, she used only the Septuagint, as did the author of our epistle. So far, so good. But a credibility gap looms and must be overcome.

Scores of allusions to the Old Testament and at least thirty direct quotations[104] adeptly chosen and arranged to underline the author's meaning, make scholars think that Hebrews was written by a Jewish theologian. If Priscilla was a Roman aristocrat, she wasn't a scholar with a lifetime of rabbinical studies. How did Priscilla learn the Old Testament so thoroughly?

She had the help of a book that grouped certain scripture by topic. According to the *testimonia* theory, the author took quotations from a testimonia book instead of hunting for them in the Bible.[105] In the book were verses about the Messiah, for example, gathered from many books of the Bible. Very useful for teaching and debate. We know the post-apostolic church had testimonia books. A nineteenth-century view supposes they were based on older documents, going back to the early church. Can we believe it? We can and must. A Dead Sea Scroll, 4Q Testimonia, is just such a document.[106]

Markus Barth analyzed numerous quotations in the first chapter of Hebrews, having to do with God's Son. They are hymns from the Old Testament, taken from psalms about the kingship of God, and His Anointed One.[107] These hymns are found in Psalms 2, 45, 97, 102, 110 and II Sam. 7. Barth says the hymns were used in Old Testament times on a specific day, probably the tabernacle festival. He adds that scripture texts in the second and third chapters of Hebrews tie in with the liturgy of the same festival. Someone collected the hymns and liturgy for use long before the Epistle. So, the author did not have to hand-pick and arrange scripture citations from the Bible.[108] A testimonia book was used.

Construction of the Epistle to the Hebrews was well within Priscilla's capability.

More About Priscilla of Rome

Having answered one question about Priscilla's scholarly qualifications, we must field another: Can a proselyte have written the Epistle to the Hebrews?

Though at home in the milieu of Jewish faith, the author need not be Jewish by birth. Only one statement hints at Jewish ancestry - Heb. 1:1 where reference is made to "our father" to whom God spoke through the prophets. This could easily have been written by one of Jewish faith, a proselyte, identifying with the religious past. In the United States, immigrants young and old, from all parts of the world, think of "our forefathers" who founded this country as their own. They do so out of a sense of identification with their present land - not because they are lineal descendants of *Mayflower* immigrants.

Priscilla knew enough about Judaism to instruct Apollos, a learned Jew, in the scripture of his faith. She was married to Aquila, a Jew, and went to Corinth with him when Claudius banished Jews from Rome. She attended the synagogue in Ephesus with Aquila (Acts 18:26). She had a ministry to many Jewish Christians, for Ephesus had a large Essene population, a group from which many of the first Christians were drawn. Jewish by birth or not, Priscilla was eminently qualified to write Heb. 1:1.

In the Epistle, I descry evidence of Roman upbringing. I have already mentioned the opinion of the author that Jewish food taboos were spiritually ineffectual for those who were led by them. The phrase referring to those who follow or once followed them hints the author may never have done so. The author calls them "strange teachings" that Hebrew Christians are to avoid.[109] Strange to whom? The readers are Hebrews. The customs are strange to the author, then.

Another clue is the dissertation on paternal discipline in Heb. 12:5-11. Who was likely to compare such discipline with the chastisement of God (Heb. 12:9)? Roman fathers were strict. Roman children were obedient. As head of the household (paterfamilias), fathers had power of life and death over every family member. Roman boys who grew up and became important people still had to obey their fathers. Fathers alone had any legal property rights.[110] Franz Poland calls paternal authority in ancient Roman families "unexampled."[111] Edith Hamilton wrote: "...What they called in Rome the *Patria Potestas*, the Father's Authority, was clearly an awful matter. There was no rebelling against it."[112]

All this applied to girls as much as to boys.[113] We have a right to say that a Roman woman, speaking in terms of her own family background and experiences, could very well compare the discipline of God with strict discipline in the home. "...For the moment all discipline seems painful rather than pleasant; later it yields the peaceful fruit of righteousness to those who have been trained by it (Heb. 12:11)."

Note the phrase "those who have been trained by it." We sense the author is writing from experience. A psalmist wrote: "As a father pities his children, so the Lord pities those who fear him" (Ps. 103:13), but a Roman was apt to write Heb. 12:5-11.

Along the same line of reasoning, it is interesting to note that only in Rome were pastors characteristically known as "rulers" or "leaders."[114] This noun appears in the thirteenth chapter of Hebrews three times, in verses 7, 17, and 24. Here is evidence that the author of Hebrews, whether Jewish by birth or not, was a resident of Rome:

> It can hardly be accidental that the only writings - whether in the New Testament or in the Apostolic Fathers - which speak of the Christian ministers bluntly as 'rulers,' are connected with Rome, where the idea of command was in the very atmosphere.[115]

Another indication of the author's connection with Rome has to do with discussion of the personage Melchizedek in chapters five and seven. Melchizedek is called a “high priest” (see Heb 5:5, 6) - terminology that appears in the ancient Roman liturgy. Such terminology may have been in the author's liturgical vocabulary, or conversely, Roman liturgy may have borrowed the author's words. In the former case, our author was likely a Roman or long-term resident of Rome. In the latter case, the author was well known and highly regarded in Rome, and by implication, a resident of Rome at one time.

M. A. R. Tuker has this to say:

> The Roman origin of the epistle, indeed, is enshrined in the Roman liturgy. In that liturgy, and in no other, the priesthood of Melchizedek is invoked, and the words used are those of the Epistle to the Hebrews *summus sacerdos Melchisedech.* Moreover, by a fluke, they are recorded in the oldest reference to the Roman canon, and must take their place by the side of the 'Amen!' of Justin as root-words of the liturgy... It formed the pivot of Prisca's reconstruction of the temple not made with hands, and it was meet it should find expression in the liturgy of the great Church she illustrated.[116]

In concluding this part of our discussion, we can say confidently that whoever wrote Hebrews was a Roman, or a long-term resident of Rome. Even the “hypothetical unknown person” who allegedly wrote Hebrews - that ghostly figure haunting our investigation - would certainly have to be a Roman ghost.

The Odd Couple?

If Priscilla was of nobler lineage than Aquila, highly educated, eminent in church leadership, were they poorly matched - an “Odd Couple”? Not necessarily, but now is a good time to focus our attention on the man she married.

Aquila hovers beneficently as we talk about Priscilla, and in every aspect of their work for Christ we sense their accord. Together they shared the adventure of rescuing Paul, alluded to in Rom. 16:3,4. Both agreed to open their home to the people they taught and cared about. When Priscilla wrote to the Hebrews - and she is now the prime suspect - Aquila filled in details she wanted to know from his own solid acquaintance with scripture.

We do not mean to asperse the happy pair when we ask: was Aquila culturally inferior to Priscilla? Priscilla's family was above him socially - but was there an intellectual and educational dissimilarity? According to Plumptre, history indicates that both Aquila and his wife "possessed in a very high degree the gifts of 'wisdom and knowledge,' that they were thoroughly imbued with (Pauline) teaching" - teaching which later became "the faith of the whole Church of Christ." Furthermore, his occupation - tentmaking - was "as in the case of St. Paul, compatible with the highest education."[117]

Notice his name. Aquila, although he was not Roman, bore the name of an illustrious Roman (Aquila Pontius, one of the murderers of Julius Caesar)[118] Possibly, he adopted the name because it was prominent. Plumptre, however, offers a different explanation:

> ... it furnishes an interesting instance at an early date of a practice that afterwards became common, that is, the adoption by Jews who were settled among the heathens of the names of *animals* ... Wolff, Bar (Bear), Hirsch (Stag), Adler (Eagle, the exact equivalent of Aquila), are familiar instances of this.[119]

Was Aquila, in fact, a freedman of Pudens, as the theory goes?[120] What can we say about his status as a freed slave, if such was the case? Statistically, there is one chance in three that he was once a slave. By the end of the third century, Rome had 400,000 slaves - about a third of the city's population.[121] Everyone with a little money had slaves. A typical Roman family owned fifteen and rich men owned hundreds.[122]

For Aquila, the odds are even higher. A native of Pontus on the Black Sea, he was a foreigner in Rome like most slaves. Many had been seized and brought to Rome in the days of Pompey (1st century B.C.). Slave expeditions to Asia systematically added to their ranks.[123]

What did slaves do? Not all were farm laborers or domestics. Educated slaves were tutors, secretaries, librarians and doctors.[124] Their status was gradually elevated in the first century. Many were given the utmost respect and consideration. Some slaves were like members of the families who owned them.[125]

Freedmen were often of high intelligence, their capability elevating them above slave status.[126] Many attained enviable social and political position. Harnack said that one of the two most powerful men in Rome at the time of Emperor Claudius was his private secretary, Narcissus - a freedman.[127]

A law enacted in 18 B.C. restricted but did not bar the marriage of freedmen into senatorial families. The law held that a child of a senator or consul or his grandchild or great-grandchild through male descent could not marry an ex-slave.[128] That is, Priscilla could marry a freedman if her maternal grandfather were a consul, but not if her paternal grandfather were a consul.

Freedmen were often related to consular families as nieces, nephews and cousins. Many children of consuls had "immensely wealthy" first cousins whose mother or father was an ex-slave.[129] For example, a freedman's son, Claudius Etruscus, was the nephew of the Consul of 83 A.D.[130]

Slavery carried no stigma. A commonplace misfortune, it could be overcome by intelligence and hard work. A slave could win respect as well as freedom.

Nor did Aquila lack social acceptability as a Jew. "Mixed marriages," such as that of Timothy's parents (Acts 16:2f), were not exceptional. In the ancient world Jews often married into leading families.[131]

Aquila's status was no bar to church responsibilities he shared with Priscilla. The early church was a model of class egalitarianism. Slaves could be teachers and high officials in the congregation, and they often were.[132]

I can give a few examples of slaves and freedmen who rose to high status in the church. Hermas, who wrote the apocryphal, "Shepherd of Hermas," was a slave.[133] His brother Pius was a Roman bishop (142-157 A.D.)[134] Another bishop of Rome was an ex-slave, Callistus (218-222 A.D.)[135]

Aquila and Priscilla could teach and preach no matter who they were. Ability and charisma were the sole criteria. And Priscilla could have written the Epistle to the Hebrews even if she were an ex-slave who had somehow learned the Bible and classical writings. An instance of a freed slave who "arrived" literarily was Tiro. Tiro was Cicero's secretary and helped him with his writings. When Cicero died, Tiro moved up to the job of guardian and editor of his literary estate.[136]

Apparently, in Corinth, Priscilla worked along with Paul and Aquila at tentmaking. Their trade did not preclude a high level of education, or even a high social position.

As for Paul and Aquila, boys in orthodox Jewish families always learned a trade. It made no difference how financially secure they were.[137] A trade was part of a self-supporting way of life. Among the well-to-do, even in non-Jewish families, a trade was insurance for the future.[138]

How did Priscilla participate in tentmaking? She helped weave tent cloth. At home, she may have supervised slaves who did the weaving. But she, too, had to learn. Weaving was part of every household. Even in wealthy homes, homespun was still being manufactured in the first century.[139] It is said that Augustus liked to wear homespun around the house and made his own family do the weaving.[140]

Tentmaking gave Aquila and Priscilla mobility as well as security. Like Paul, they were enabled to re-locate, by choice or necessity.[141] So in Corinth we see them making sails for ships. In Ephesus, they made luxurious tents and marquees.[142]

Work was plentiful in Ephesus.[143] A good place for Aquila and his wife to settle, to build up the church. As a matter of fact, they were there for a long time. In 65 or 66 A.D., their concern for the Hebrews Christians of Ephesus would lead Priscilla to write the Epistle.

Interim Summary

"The greatest friend of truth is Time..." wrote Charles Caleb Coulton, with keen historical sense. The truth about Priscilla and her family was literally dug out of the earth but not until the eighteenth and nineteenth centuries. Harnack's theory about Priscilla followed in 1900, a long time after the writing of Hebrews.

For centuries the letter was attributed to one man or another, typically by way of casual guesswork. Now several suspected authors have been dismissed from the line-up, including the only serious contender among them, Apollos. In the next chapter, we shall see how the Dead Sea Scrolls, discovered in modern times, illuminate the mystery.

Where does Priscilla stand now?

She has a star pupil, Apollos, who can prove from scripture that Jesus is the Messiah. This is to be an underlying theme of Hebrews. Unlike her student, she was converted by one who saw and heard Jesus (Heb. 2:3).

She knows Philo, who will influence the terminology of Hebrews.

At last she is re-united with her family in the upper stratum of Roman society.

She is grounded in literature, philosophy and rhetoric.

Eloquent like Apollos, she preaches the gospel. Fervent in spirit like him, (Acts 18:25), she has given up luxury and noble status for trials - and high adventure - with Christ. These traits will be mirrored in Hebrews.

Priscilla stands in Timothy's circle (Heb. 13:23), as a corollary of her close friendship with Paul.

Her marriage to Aquila is reasonable as well as congenial, and they share a ministry in Rome, Corinth and Ephesus.

Pen and papyrus in hand, Priscilla is ready to write a letter.

On her desk is a *testimonia* book to aid her.

Destination? Ephesus!

*Family Tree of the Acilii Glabriones**

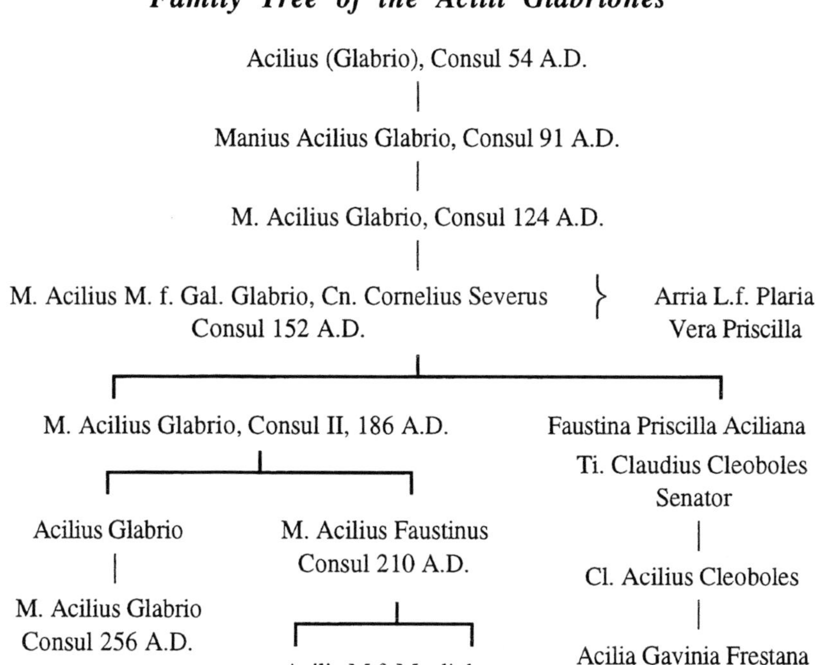

**Paulys Real-Encyclopadie der Classischen Altertumswissenschaft.* Vol. I. (Stuttgart: J.B. Metzlerscher Verlag, 1894), p. 258.

NOTES TO CHAPTER VI

1. Chrysostom, *Homily on the Acts of the Apostles. Nicene and Post-Nicene Fathers of the Christian Church*, Vol. XI. ed., Philip Schaff. (New York: The Christian Literature Co., 1889), p. 246, note 2 quoting *Serm. in illud Salutate Prisc et Aquil*, Vol. iii, p. 176B. See Herbert Lockyer, *All the Men of the Bible*. (Grand Rapids: Zondervan Publishing Co., 1952), p. 52.

2. Harnack, *The Mission and Expansion of Christianity in the First Three Centuries*, tr. and ed., James Moffatt, Vol. 2. Second, enlarged and revised edition. (New York: G. P. Putnam's Sons and London: Williams and Norgate, 1908), p. 68.

3. Antoinette Clark Wire, *The Corinthian Women Prophets* (Minneapolis: Fortress Press, 1990), p. 210 appendix 5.

4. Harnack, *ZNW* 1900, Vol. I, p. 34-35.

5. Donald Wayne Riddle, "Early Christian Hospitality: A Factor in the Gospel Tradition," *Journal of Biblical Literature* vol. LVII, (Philadelphia: Soc of Biblical Literature, 1938), p. 151.

6. George A. Barton, *The Apostolic Age*. (Philadelphia: University of Pennsylvania Press, 1936), p. 71.

7. Acts 18:2,3; 18:18,19; 18:24-26; Rom. 16:3,4; I Cor. 16:19; and II Tim. 4:19.

8. Chrysostom commented on Priscilla's pre-eminence in Acts 18:18; Acts 18:26; Rom. 16:3; and II Tim. 4:19.

9. E. H. Plumptre, "Aquila and Priscilla," *Biblical Studies*, E.H. Plumptre, ed. (London: Griffith, Farran, Okeden and Welch, 1885), p. 422-425; also G. Edmundson, *The Church in Rome in the First Century* (London: Longmans, 1913), p. 11-12.

10. Claudius' edict is variously dated 49-52 A.D. Spence-Jones favors 49 A.D. Suetonius, writing in the second century, has 52 A.D. (Henry Bettenson, Documents of the Christian Church. New York and London: Oxford Univ. Press, 9th printing, 1961, p. 4 quoting Suetonius, *Vita Claudii*, xxxv.4.)

11. Verna J. Dozier and James R. Adams, *Brothers and Sisters* (Boston: Cowley Publications, 1993), p. 89.

12. Edmundson, *op. cit.*, p. 22.

13. *Ibid.*, note 2.

14. Edmundson, p. 13, note 4.

15. Wikenhauser, p. 399.

16. H. D. M. Spence-Jones, *The Early Christians in Rome*. (London: Methuen & Co., Ltd., 1910), p. 5.

17. Ben Witherington III, *Women in the Earliest Churches*, (Cambridge: Cambridge University Press, 1988), citing E. Haenchen, p. 153.

18. Morton, *op. cit.*, p. 349.

19. Eusebius, *op. cit.*, p. 105.

20. Spence-Jones, *op. cit.*, p. 14.

21. *Ibid.*

22. Spence-Jones, p. vii.

23. Morton, p. 470 and Spence-Jones, p. 263.

24. William Thomas Walsh, *Saint Peter the Apostle*. (New York: The Macmillan Co., 1948), p. 280.

25. M. A. R. Tuker and Hope Malleson, *Handbook to Christian and Ecclesiastical Rome, Part I, The Christian Monuments of Rome* (London: Adam and Charles Black, 1900), p. 495.

26. H. V. Morton, *op. cit.*, p. 471.

27. *Dictionnaire d'archeologie chretienne et de liturgie (DACL)*, p. 1877,1878. translated by Julie E. Johnson.

28. *Oxford Dictionary of the Christian Church*, p. 919.

29. Translation by Leonard E. Boyle. Joan Morris, *The Lady Was a Bishop: The Hidden History of Women with Clerical Ordination and the Jurisdiction of Bishops*. (New York: The Macmillan Company; London: Collier-Macmillan Limited, 1973), p. 121; 171, note 18.

30. Vat. lat. 9698, p. 78. Courtesy of Bibliothèque Nationale de France.

31. *The Catholic Encyclopedia*, Vol. XII (New York: The Gilmary Society and the Encyclopedia Press, Inc., 1913), p. 428.

32. Priscilla is the familiar, diminutive form of Prisca. The church bears the inscription: "Titulus Aquila et Prisca." See Edith Deen, *All of the Women of the Bible*. (New York: Harper & Bros., Publishers, 1955), p. 229.

33. Joseph Holzner, *Paul of Tarsus*. tr. Frederic C. Eckhoff (St. Louis, MO., and London: Herder & Co., 1944), p. 424 and Spence-Jones, *op. cit.,* p. 262.

34. Holzner, *op. cit.*, p. 424.

35. Spence-Jones, p. 262.

36. Wm. Ingraham Kip, *The Catacombs of Rome*. (New York: Daniel Dana, Jr., 1863), p. 51.

37. Spence-Jones, p. 265.

38. *Ibid.*, p. 267.

39. Edmundson, p. 252
40. Bettenson, p. 120
41. Edmundson, p. 52
42. Spence-Jones, p. 267
43. *Ibid.*, p. 12.
44. *Ibid.*, p. 271
45. *Ibid.*, p. 272. Spence-Jones cites the reservoir as a unique feature of the Priscilla Catacomb. Maitland mentions that wells were dug in certain catacombs (*Church in the Catacombs*, p. 29).
46. Spence-Jones, p. 267.
47. Eusebius, p. 78. (Quoting Josephus, *Antiquities* XVIII,viii,1.)
48. Eusebius, p. 95.
49. Eusebius, p. 89.
50. Nairne, *op,. cit.* p. lv and C.D. Yonge, tr., *The Works of Philo Complete and Unabridged, New Updated Edition*, Foreword by David M. Scholer (Peabody, Mass: Hendrickson Publishers, 1993), p. xiv. See also Hayes, *op. cit.*, p. 41-48.
51. Spence-Jones, p. 265.
52. Holzner, *op. cit.*, p. 424.
53. Tuker and Malleson, *Handbook to Christian and Ecclesiastical Rome* Part I, p. 495.
54. Letter from Joan Morris, 2/13/72 and Orazio Marucchi, *Le Catacombe Romane*, p. 465.
55. Edmundson, p. 278 Appendices Note f.
56. Joan Morris, letter 2/13/72. See also Edmundson p. 277.
57. Edmundson, p. 22 note 1.
58. Spence-Jones, p. 267.
59. Ludwig Hertling and Englebert Kirschbaum, *The Roman Catacombs and Their Martyrs*. tr. M. Joseph Costelloe. (U.S. The Bruce Publishing Co., 1956), p. 25.
60. *Rome in Brief.* (Guidebook to Rome) Ente Provinciale Per Il Turismo Di Roma, Via Parigi II. (Rome: Vecchioni & Guadagno, 1967), P. 7.
61. Holzner, p. 424.
62. Spence-Jones, p. 265.
63. *Ibid.*, p. 270.

64. Hertling, *op. cit.*, p. 27.

65. Franz Poland et al., *The Culture of Ancient Rome and Greece.* John Henry Freese. (London: George Harrap & Co., Ltd., 1926), p. 293, 294.

66. *The Catholic Encyclopedia*, Vol. XII, p. 428.

67. Hertling, *op. cit.*, p. 27.

68. The Hypogeum is a large room or crypt, a flight of stairs, and a large corridor at right angles to the crypt. Herling, p. 200

69. Hertling, p. 27. See genealogical chart p. 115 this book.

70. Morton, p. 348.

71. J. A. Thompson, *The Bible and Archeology*. (Grand Rapids: Wm. B. Eerdman's Publishing Co., 1962), p. 315.

72. Plumptre, E. H., *op. cit.*, p. 422.

73. *Ibid.*, p. 423. See also Edmundson, p. 11,12.

74. Edmundson, p. 243.

75. Charles Maitland, *The Church in the Catacombs*. (London: Longman, Brown, Green and Longmans, 1846), p. 12. 76.

76. Spence-Jones, p. 270.

77. *Ibid.*

78. Hertling, *op. cit.*, p. 200.

79. Spence-Jones, p. 269.

80. *Ibid.*

81. Spence-Jones, p. 270.

82. *Ibid.*, p. 269.

83. *The Catholic Encyclopedia* Vol. VI., p. 575.

84. Robert Payne, *The Horizon Book of Ancient Rome*. (New York: American Heritage Publishing Co., 1966), p. 125.

85. *Ibid.*, p. 226.

86. Poland, *op. cit.*, p. 300.

87. Payne, *op. cit.*, p. 226.

88. Poland, p. 299.

89. Payne, p. 175.

90. Judith P. Hallett, *Fathers and Daughters in Roman Society (Women and the Elite Family)*. (Princeton, New Jersey: Princeton University Press, 1984), p.

108, 164, citing Cicero, *Brutus* 239 and E. S. Gruen, *The Last Generation of the Roman Republic* (Berkeley, Los Angeles, and London, 1974).

91. Price, *op. cit.*, p. 178.

92. Elsie Thomas Culver, *Women in the World of Religion.* (New York: Doubleday & Co., 1967), p. 57.

93. Deen, *op. cit.*, p. 229.

94. Culver, p. 60.

95. For a good, brief discussion pro and con, see Peake, *A Critical Introduction to the New Testament*, p. 41-44.

96. *The Interpreter's Dictionary of the Bible* Vol. IV. (New York, Nashville: Abingdon Press, 1962), p. 112.

97. Morton, *op. cit.*, p. 348.

98. Spence-Jones, p. 270.

99. Jean Daniélou, *The Dead Sea Scrolls and Primitive Christianity.* Tr. Salvatore Attanasio. (Baltimore: Helicon Press, Inc., 1958), p. 126.

100. Holzner, *op. cit.*, p. 420.

101. Spence-Jones, p. 5.

102. Holzner, p. 421.

103. Daniélou, *op. cit.*, p. 126.

104. Markus Barth, "The Old Testament in Hebrews, an essay in Biblical Hermeneutics," *Current Issues in New Testament Interpretation: Essays in Honor of Otto A. Piper.* ed. Wm. Klassen and Graydon F. Snyder. (New York: Harper & Bros., 1962), 54.

105. *Ibid.*, p. 73. Canon F. C. Synge (*Hebrews and the Scriptures*, London, 1959, p. 17, 53ff.), Burkitt, Harris, Dodd and Allegro support the testimonia theory.

106. Allegro, *op. cit.*, p. 138,139 and Barth, *op. cit.*, 268, 269.

107. Barth, *op. cit.*, p. 72.

108. *Ibid.*, p. 173

109. "Do not be led away by diverse and strange teachings; for it is well that the heart be strengthened by grace, not by foods, which have not benefited their adherents." (Heb. 13:9 RSV)

110. Poland, *op. cit.*, p. 251.

111. *Ibid.*

112. Edith Hamilton, *The Roman Way.* Copyright 1932 by W. W. Norton & Company, Inc.; copyright renewed 1960 by Edith Hamilton. Reprinted in

Everyday Life in Ancient Times. Wash., D.C.: National Geographic Soc., 1951, 6th printing, 1964, p. 269.

113. J. P. V. D. Balsdon, *Roman Women: Their History and Habits*. (New York: The John Day Co., 1963), p. 45.

114. Attridge., *op. cit.*, p. 391.

115. Burnett Hillman Streeter, *The Primitive Church*. (New York: The Macmillan Company, 1929), p. 205.

116. Tuker, "The Gospel According to Prisca," *op. cit.*, p. 98.

117. Plumptre, *op. cit.*, p. 418.

118. *Ibid.*

119. *Ibid.*, p. 426

120. Spence-Jones, p. 270

121. Payne, *op. cit.*, p. 273. This was double the estimated slave population in the late republic (1st century B.C.).

122. Holzner, *op. cit.*, p. 425.

123. Thompson, *op. cit.*, p. 315.

124. Payne, p. 159.

125. *Ibid.*, p. 273.

126. Poland, *op. cit.*, p. 294.

127. Holzner, *op. cit.*, p. 425 referring to Harnack, *Die Mission und Ausbretung des Christentums*, 4th ea., Leipzig, 1924.

128. Balsdon, *op. cit.*, p. 175.

129. *Ibid.*

130. *Ibid.*, p. 312.

131. Sir. W. M. Ramsay, *The Bearing of recent Discoveries on the Trustworthiness of the New Testament*. (London: Hodder & Stoughton, 1915), p. 357.

132. Spence-Jones, p. 136.

133. *Ibid.*

134. *Ibid.*

135. *Ibid.*

136. Payne, *op. cit.*, p. 159.

137. Morton, *op. cit.*, p. 9.

138. A. Powell Davies, *The First Christian.* (New York: Farrar, Straus and Cudahy, 1956), p. 16.

139. Balsdon, *op. cit.*, p. 270.

140. *Ibid.*

141. Davies, *op. cit.*, p. 16.

142. Morton, p. 380.

143. *Ibid.*

CHAPTER SEVEN

DESTINATION: EPHESUS

Beyond reasonable doubt, the destination of Hebrews was Ephesus, capital of the Roman province of Asia. One reason is strikingly obvious. A clue in the postscript has Timothy anxious to return to the readers (Heb. 13:23). Where but to Ephesus - the locale of his ministry - would Timothy be returning? Paul urged him to remain there to combat false teaching that menaced the church (I Tim. 1:3,4).

Staking out Ephesus, we see how the city meets all conditions for being home to the first recipients of Hebrews. No other city meets all these conditions. Road signs pointing to Ephesus will not take the traveller/detective to Jerusalem, Alexandria, Antioch, Corinth or Rome.

Instead of a profile of the author, we now construct a profile of City X, home of the addressees. Look at the *Fact Comparison Chart for Churches in 65 A.D.* Read the description of City X in six categories, and solve for "X". That is, match one of six major centers of church activity with City X. This is how the stakeout will proceed.

People of the City

Look at section 1 of the chart: "People of the City." Population statistics are given. Both the total populace and the Jewish community should be numerous to match City X, addressed in Hebrews. It isn't hard to see why. The gospel was planted strategically in big cities, from where it spread to outlying districts. Timothy and Paul worked mainly in the population centers. Whoever wrote Hebrews was closely related to them. In fact, many points of contact with Paul's writings reflected in Hebrews led Spicq to dub the author "Paul's spiritual alumnus."[1] Coordination of plans with Timothy (Heb. 13:23) makes the author a coworker of

Timothy (and Paul). As their coworker, this individual urged people to keep the faith in what must have been a key city of the ancient world.

City X had a sizable Jewish colony. If the readers were simply Jews, it would be more complicated to pinpoint the locale. But the letter was sent to former Essenes. So all cities without a major Essene colony are out. By this test, Corinth and Rome are disqualified. Jerusalem, Alexandria, and Antioch will be eliminated for other reasons.

Glance over the first section to see which city best matches population statistics for City X. Ephesus, with 250,000 persons, ranks fourth in total population. Only Rome, Alexandria and Antioch were more populous in the first century. Cosmopolitan Ephesus had a major Essene colony. Only here do we find specific mention of disciples of John the Baptist, whose religious outlook took root in this Asian metropolis. He was akin to the Essene sect.[2] Raymond Brown notes that Paul's letters to or from Ephesus were influenced by Qumran (Essene) literature.[3] Scanning the first section, we see that Alexandria too had a large Essene colony. There is no doubt that Jews were numerous in Alexandria, for they occupied two of the city's five residential areas. Philo and other sources witness that of these Jews, many were Essenes. More about Alexandria when evidence is summarized.

People of the Church

We expect the people of the church to be a fair cross section of the people of the city. They are, with the possible exception of mysterious Alexandria, for which there is a provocative dearth of information. Ephesus, Jerusalem and Antioch had Essene converts. Corinth had very few. We deduce from Paul's letter to the Romans that of the Jewish Christians in Rome, most were not former Essenes. He did not argue within the framework of Essene doctrine.

Former Essenes predominated in Church X. This does not mean Gentile converts were scarce in City X or Church X. It means only that the author's ministry was largely, if not chiefly, to Hebrew Christians.[4] The author addressed Hebrews, who wavered between their new faith and the lure of their old faith.

Who were the readers? This used to be the subject of sundry speculation. A nineteenth-century scholar, E. M. Roeth, swept past the title and subject matter of the letter to propose in 1836 that Hebrews was addressed mainly to Gentiles, or simply to all Christians.[5] He won impressive followers.[6] Then, publication of the contents of the Dead Sea Scrolls in the 1950's led to the startling discovery that Hebrews was written in the context of Qumran thought.[7] Of all New Testament writing, Hebrews gives the most comprehensive reply to certain doctrines of the Qumran Sect.[8] Spicq argued convincingly that Hebrews was written for Essene-Christian readers, who were somehow related to Qumran.[9]

Today, scholars still disagree on the locale. Bowman places the destination in Samaria near Sychar.[10] But he does so on the premise that Essene converts regrouped there after Stephen's martyrdom in Jerusalem. Spicq favors Syria. Braun prefers Asia Minor where Ephesus is located. And Leonhard Goppelt claims Rome, while the majority favor Alexandria.[11] On what grounds? Former Essenes lived there. Although I believe the specific locale must be Ephesus, their premise is valid.

With discovery of the Dead Sea Scrolls, Essenes - a sect of Judaism contemporary with the Pharisees and Sadducees have come into sharp focus. Since most of the scrolls are from the first century B.C. and early first century, the group that wrote or copied them stood on the threshhold of the emergence of Christianity.

Three writers of the first century detailed their importance: Flavius Josephus, historian of *The Jewish War* and *The Antiquities of the Jews*; Philo, the Alexandrian philosopher, and Pliny the Elder, a Roman author (*Natural History*). Philo, like Josephus and Pliny, admired the Essenes, who exemplified the thesis of his book, *Every Good Man is Free*.[12]

FACT - COMPARISON CHART FOR CHURCHES IN 65 A.D.

CITY

"X" DESCRIBED IN HEBREWS	EPHESUS	JERUSALEM	ALEXANDRIA	ANTIOCH	CORINTH	ROME
PEOPLE OF THE CITY						
Numerous; Sizeable Jewish - Essene colony.	Population ca 250,000; Cosmopolitan; Many Jews; Major Essene colony.	Essenes and other Jews	Population 700,000 (half slave). Very many Jews and Essenes.	Population 500,000; Josephus estimates 50,000 Jews	Romans; Greeks; Syrians; many Jews, Egyptians	Population 1,000,000 (one-third slave) 30-50,000 Jews
PEOPLE OF THE CHURCH						
Converts from Essenic - Judaism are addressed.	Former Essenes and many Gentile converts; largest ratio of converts to total population.	Former Essenes and other Jews	Unknown	Many Jewish-Christian refugees from Palestine.	Predominantly Gentile.	A few thousand at most; predominantly Gentile; many Jews; some former Essenes
MODE OF CONVERSION						
By eyewitnesses to the ministry of Jesus	John the Apostle; John the elder; Migrants from Palestine; Paul, Timothy, Priscilla and Aquila.	Jesus, apostles, disciples	Unknown; tradition that Mark evangelized.	Apostles; refugees from Palestine.	Paul the founder; Peter, Apollos	Peter; refugees from Palestine
ORGANIZATION AND LEADERSHIP						
Well-organized; many conscientious leaders who replaced the earlier ones	Well-organized native ministry replaced the apostles and founders. Leaders worked well with Paul.	Well-organized native ministry.	Unknown	Looked to Jerusalem for leadership	Depended on outside leadership (mainly Rome) to settle disputes	Strong leadership

FACT - COMPARISON CHART FOR CHURCHES IN 65 A.D.
(continued)

CITY

"X" DESCRIBED IN HEBREWS	EPHESUS	JERUSALEM	ALEXANDRIA	ANTIOCH	CORINTH	ROME
SPIRITUAL CONDITION						
Signs and wonders at first. Fervor has given way to apathy. Good works and generosity continue. Threat of reversion to former beliefs.	Signs and wonders converted many in early days. Enthusiasm has given way to apathy, but good works and generosity continue. False teachings resisted.	Influence of legalistic Judaism remained strong. Evangelistic center.	Unknown	Evangelistic center	Abundance of spiritual gifts; factionalism	Renowned for their faith (Rom. 1:8); doctrinal disputes between Jewish and Gentile converts
PERSECUTION ENCOUNTERED BY CHRISTIANS						
Subject to derision and robbery (and some may have been imprisoned) at first, but none had died for their faith.	Local anti-Christian sentiment for economic reasons. Demetrius provoked a riot in the early days.	Stephen's martyrdom followed by persecution and imprisonment of Christians. James the Righteous martyred 62 A.D.	Unknown	Some had fled persecution in Palestine	Threatened by Neronian persecution. Social conflict with Paganism.	Persecuted almost from the beginning. Severe Neronian persecution 64-65 A.D. Many martyrs.

It was Pliny who revealed that Essenes were grouped on the western bank of the Dead Sea.[13] Their proximity to the Dead Sea, and many crucial identities with sectarian scrolls found in the vicinity have linked the Essenes inexorably to Qumran. Recent challenges to a predominantly Essenic presence at Qumran are sparsely defended and inconsequential to the well-documented existence of an Essene community.

Nonetheless, one should be aware of recent claims that the group at Qumran was Sadducean in origin - premising that typical Sadducean beliefs, absent at Qumran, were jettisoned. James C. Vanderkam, defending the dominant view, points out that Pliny and other ancient sources had no reason to fabricate their reports about the Essenes. Furthermore, their descriptions match sectarian texts: literature from the Qumran library "is showing us an actual Essene group."[14]

The Readers were Former Essenes

The readers were former Essenes. I do not aim to present all the evidence, which has steadily amassed since H. Kosmala first stated the case. A few highlights will suffice. Four themes common to Hebrews and Essenism will be discussed:

1. People of the New Covenant
   (Dialogue with the Essene Self-Image)
2. High Priest, Sacrifice and Atonement
3. Angles on Angels
4. One Messiah or Two?
   (A Priestly Messiah?)

A word of encouragement is in order; pay close attention and you will be rewarded with a better understanding of the Epistle to the Hebrews.

PEOPLE OF THE NEW COVENANT

(Dialogue with Essene Self-Image)

How did the men and women of Qumran describe themselves? They were people of the "Covenant" - specifically, the "New Covenant."[15] There are twenty-eight references to the "New Covenant" in the New Testament. *Of these, exactly one half are in Hebrews.*[16] Both the sect at Qumran and the author of Hebrews cite the covenant theme in Jeremiah (Jer. 31:31-34, quoted in Heb. 8:8-12) and allude to the "blood of the covenant" (Zech. 9:11).

The Sect thought of themselves as recipients of a New Covenant.[17] Of many instances, I cite two:

> And all who come into the order of the community shall pass over into the covenant before God...(Manual of Discipline)[18]

> .....those who acted treacherously against the new covenant, for they did not believe the covenant of God...(The Habakkuk Commentary)[19]

The Epistle to the Hebrews reminded former Essenes in sledge-hammer fashion that *Christians* are the people of the New Covenant:

> Therefore he (Jesus) is the mediator of a new covenant...(Heb. 9:15).

> .....and to Jesus, the mediator of a new covenant...(Heb. 12:24).

> This makes Jesus the surety of a better covenant. (Heb. 7:22).

We know Habakkuk was close to the heart of the Sect, for a Commentary on the Old Testament book was found in the Qumran caves. The author of Hebrews used a quotation from Habakkuk when admonishing readers to hold fast to the new covenant:

> For yet a little while,
> and the coming one shall come and
> shall not tarry;
> but my righteous one shall live by faith,
> and if he shrinks back,
> my soul has no pleasure in him.
>
> (Heb. 10:37,38 quoting Habakkuk 2:3,4)

The author follows with an exhortation:

> but we are not of those who shrink back and are destroyed,
> but those who have faith and keep their souls. (Heb. 10:39)

Now compare this from Qumran:

> With the coming of day and night
> I will enter the Covenant of God
> And with the outgoing of evening and morning
> I will speak his decrees;
> And while they exist I will set my limit
> So that I may not turn back.
>
> (From the Closing Psalm in the
> Manual of Discipline)[20]

Both the sect and our author believe that turning away from it is to break the covenant with God (Heb. 10:39). They use similar words: "We are not of those who shrink back"; "I may not turn back (from the covenant)."

HIGH PRIEST, SACRIFICE AND ATONEMENT

To the writer of Hebrews, Jesus is Messiah and High Priest. He is High Priest of an eternal order - comparable, as we have seen, to Melchizedek:

> ... not according to a legal requirement concerning bodily descent but by the power of an indestructible life. For it is witnessed of him, "Thou art a priest for ever, after the order of Melchizedek"
> (Heb. 7:16,17, quoting Ps. 110:4).

Unlike other High Priests, Christ entered into the true sanctuary - Heaven itself (Heb. 9:24). Offering himself, not the blood of bulls and goats,

> ...Christ...offered for all time a single sacrifice for sins...
> (Heb. 10:12).

Efficacious, his once-and-for-all sacrifice need not be repeated (Heb. 7:27).

The Christian life is a continuous "Day of Atonement"[21] (when a bullock and two goats were sacrificed as a sin offering).[22] But instead of repeating the usual sacrifice, we "continually offer up a sacrifice of praise to God, that is, the fruit of lips that acknowledge his name" (Heb. 13:15).

How does all this show a dialogue with typical Essene thought? After all, the Essenes did not invent sacrifice and atonement. These, along with the High Priesthood, were vital themes in Judaism.

As Bowman indicates, Qumran lacked a Day of Atonement. Hebrews' teaching on a "continuous Day of Atonement" emphasizes the lack (Heb. 10:19-31; 12:22-24; 13:12-16). And the unique High Priest of Hebrews, who sacrificed himself, clashes with the Qumran High Priest of Aaronic descent who expounds scripture and leads the congregation. The nature of the High Priesthood was in the foreground of Qumran teaching. So Bowman is sure Hebrews was written in the context of Qumran, contemporaneous with the Sect.[23]

I find explicit proof for this in the thirteenth chapter of Hebrews. The author writes about Jesus' sacrifice:

> So Jesus also suffered outside the gate in order to sanctify the people through his own blood. Therefore let us go forth to him outside the camp...
>
> (Heb. 13:12,13).

The sacrifice (crucifixion) took place outside the camp (outside the city). This is different from the usual sacrifice that takes place in the Temple (Lev. 16:16). The animals are killed in the sanctuary. On the Day of Atonement, their blood is brought into the Holy of Holies. Later, the bodies of the sacrificed animals are burned outside the camp (Lev. 16:27). The author compares the sin offering outside the camp with the sin offering in the sanctuary, and says the one outside the camp is better:

> We have an altar from which those who serve the tent (tabernacle) have no right to eat. For the bodies of those animals whose blood is brought into the sanctuary by the high priest as a sacrifice for sin are burned outside the camp. So Jesus also suffered outside the gate in order to sanctify the people through his own blood
>
> (Heb. 13:10-12).

How do we know the author is writing in the context of Qumran? Well, their most common sacrifice was a red heifer as a sin offering (Num. Ch. 19). This heifer was slain outside the camp.[24] *Not in the sanctuary.* Jesus was *slain outside the camp* - a fact meaningful to former Essenes, but not so meaningful to other Jews, for whom the sacrifices in the sanctuary were far more important.

Why was the sacrifice of the red heifer customary in Qumran? The Essenes were self-excluded from the Temple. By law, only certain sacrifices were permitted away from the Temple sanctuary. These were called "lustral" ones, for "cleansing." The heifer was not only a sin offering. Its ashes were needed to prepare Holy Water, for purifying.[25]

The Holy Water was for ritual washings, so frequent among Essenes.[26] An allusion to their common practice is found in Hebrews:

> ...our hearts sprinkled clean from an evil conscience and our bodies washed with pure water...
>
> (Heb. 10:22).

ANGLES ON ANGELS

Reading through the Epistle to the Hebrews, one is struck by an oddity. The entire first two chapters are devoted to establishing the superiority of Christ to angels. Indeed, as we shall see, the author is impelled to explain why Christ had not come to earth as an angel. How do we account for the prominence of this unusual line of reasoning? In fact, this is one more area of dialogue with Essene beliefs.

To the Sect, angels were in the foreground of God's plan. They were myriad spirits; some good, some bad. A few comments on bad angels in the Qumran documents:

> And in the hand of the angel of darkness is all dominion over the sons of error ...
> And by the angel of darkness ...
> ...all destroying angels...
>
> (Manual of Discipline II).[27]

> And on the day that the man obligates himself to return to the law of Moses the angel of enmity will depart from behind him if he makes good his words
>
> (The Damascus Document XX).[28]

> ... by all the angels of destruction...
>
> (The Damascus Document II).[29]

There are good angels, too. In the apocalyptic "War of the Sons of Light with the Sons of Darkness" they fight with the army of the righteous. Of their number Raphael, Michael and Gabriel are named.[30] "The army of the holy ones," "congregation of the sons of heaven," "the eternal assembly," are other ways of describing them.[31]

You can easily discern a verbal parallel in Hebrews:[32]

> But you have come to Mount Zion and to the city of the living God, the heavenly Jerusalem, and to innumerable angels in festal gathering, and to the assembly of the first-born...
>
> (Heb. 12:22,23).

To their good angels, Qumran imputed divine powers. The Manual of Discipline boasts of a council of angels with insight into God's wisdom:

> He will purge by His truth all the deeds of Men ... to give the upright insight into the knowledge of the Most High and into the wisdom of the sons of Heaven, to give the perfect the way of understanding.[33]

The "sons of heaven" are angels in the divine council, who are in on God's "plan of operation."[34] The spirit (or angel)[35] of truth helps people to believe in the "*works of God.*"[36] When Jesus' disciples asked him, "What must we do, to be doing *the works of God?*", they were using the same phrase (John 6:28). Jesus told them: "This is *the work of God*, that you believe in him whom He has sent" (John 6:29).[37] This brief dialogue hints at a real *conflict between the role of angels and the primacy of Christ.* Angels, in Qumran thought, give help, wisdom, virtue and good works to the faithful:

> ...but the God of Israel and his angel of truth have helped all the sons of light
>
> (Manual of Discipline II).[38]

No wonder the primacy of Christ had to be established at the outset. As chapters one and two take up the challenge point by point, we read:

> (Christ is) superior to the angels.
>
> (Heb. 1:4)

> For to what angel did God ever say, "Thou art my Son..."
>
> (Heb. 1:5)

> Of the angels he says, "Who makes his angels winds (spirits) and his servants flames of fire." But of the Son he says, ... "the righteous scepter is the scepter of thy kingdom".
>
> (Heb. 1:7, 8)

> ...to what angel has he ever said, "Sit at my right hand..."
>
> (Heb. 1:13)

In fact, angels are not even superior to humankind, to whom God subjected the world (Heb. 2:5-8). To former Essenes, who thought Jesus should have come as an angel, the author said: "God is not concerned with angels, but with people. So Christ had to be made like his brothers and sisters, to be their high priest, and expiate their sins" (paraphrase, Heb. 2:16-17).

Here we have an explanation that Christ did not come to help angels, but people; therefore he had to be incarnate as a human that we might have a true model and redeemer. And we have a reason for the explanation; the author was engaging in dialogue with beliefs that were competitive and contradictory to Christianity.

The angel motif, however, is found in Hebrews, and not completely repudiated. Like the Sect at Qumran,[39] and a certain branch of contemporaneous Jewish theology, the author espouses the view that angels gave Moses the Law:

> For if the message declared by angels was valid and every transgression or disobedience received a just retribution...
>
> (Heb. 2:2).

A view, by the way, that is based on the Hebrew text, of Angel mediation of the Law[40] is assumed in Stephen's speech (Acts 7:38, 53), one of many striking points of similarity with the Damascus Document (V,18) of the Essenes,[41] which asserts that Moses received his authority from an angel. The author of Hebrews, familiar only with the Septuagint, is, like Stephen, alluding to Essene beliefs.

ONE MESSIAH OR TWO?
(A PRIESTLY MESSIAH?)

Peculiar beliefs about Covenant, Sacrifice, and Angels were recast to conform with Christian teaching. Incrementally, we perceive in Hebrews a dialogue with former Essenes; another journey to the caves of Qumran with their trove of scrolls should settle it. Once more, we superimpose the mental landscape of Qumran on that of Hebrews, for another match.

What did the average Jew believe in Jesus' day? A Messiah was bound to come soon. Woven through the New Testament is their expectancy. Unlike other Jews, Essenes had a distinctive dogma. Not one but two Messiahs were to come:[42] a Priest of the line of Aaron and a King of the line of David.[43] This is the preponderance of evidence. Our discussion will encompass recent challenges to the prevailing view.

Hearkening to the messianic dualism of Qumran, Hebrews insists that King and Priest would be combined in one person.[44] This in brief is the main reason scholars see in Hebrews a dialogue with Essenism.

The need to refute and convince is paramount. One third of the Epistle is given over to this argument- chapters five through eight. The author begins an explanation (Heb. 5:1-10), then warns it is hard to understand, but most necessary (Heb. 5:11-6:20). The core of the case is in chapter seven. In chapter eight we are told the superior priesthood of Christ typifies the new covenant, as the old priesthood of the Aaronic line typifies the old covenant.

Let's zero in on the controversy.

Documents from Qumran[45] speak of two Messiahs. The Messiah Priest of the line of Aaron is first in rank.[46] At the Messianic Banquet, the Priest with his followers are to be seated first. The Messiah of Israel (of the line of David) then enters with his followers. The Priest is first to touch the wine and bread.[47]

Non-Essene Jews looked for a Messiah of the House of David, and Jesus was identified by the church as the Davidic Messiah.[48] They did not expect their Messiah to be a priest. The writer of Hebrews, explaining the priesthood of Christ, did not address them.

At first, Essene converts to Christianity may have accepted Jesus as the Davidic Messiah. Then, disavowing his subordinate role, they placed him in the role of Priest.[49] But Jesus was of non-priestly descent. The problem is stated in Hebrews:

> For it is evident that our Lord was descended from Judah, and in connection with that tribe Moses said nothing about priests
>
> (Heb. 7:14).

How can this be reconciled? The author has an explanation. Jesus is not of the order of Aaron; he is a priest of the order of Melchizedek (Heb. 6:20; 7:11).[50] Melchizedek is an eternal figure, without mother or father; he is outside of birth and death (Heb. 7:3). By this, the status of Jesus transcends and nullifies the need for Aaronic descent.

"Melchizedek, king of Salem," as we know, means: "king of righteousness, king of peace" (Heb. 7:1,2). He is both priest and king. Jesus is patterned after him. What a superb analogy! Herein, Jesus combines the function of the two Messiahs.[51]

Does the author have a Biblical basis for this comparison? Yes, and here it is:

> The Lord says to my Lord;
> Sit at my right hand...(Ps. 110:1)
> The Lord has sworn
> and will not change his mind,
> "You are a priest for ever
> after the order of Melchizedek" (Ps. 110:4)
>
> (quoted in Heb. 5:6; 7:17; 7:21)

A text in the Old Testament abets the premise that the Messiah is a single person:[52]

> Behold, the man whose name is the Branch; for he shall grow up in his place, and he shall build the temple of the Lord, and shall bear royal honor, and shall sit and rule upon his throne. And there shall be a priest by his throne, (The Septuagint reads: "and shall be priest at his right hand"[53] and peaceful understanding shall be between them both.
>
> (Zech. 6:12,13).

The author does not fail to allude to this passage (Heb. 3:3,6). We must agree with Bowman and many others that Hebrews aims to confute the Essene claim.[54]

A recently published scroll, 4Q521, dating most likely from 100 B.C. to 70 A.D., and dubbed "The Messiah of Heaven and Earth," has been studied by Wise and Tabor.[55] They propose a translation of the text giving a single Messiah. However, Edward Cook notes that an alternate translation of the Hebrew text, giving plural Messiahs, is equally defensible, and even preferable.[56] Wise and Tabor, he says, overlooked the parallelism of the first two lines, rendering:

> (...the hea)vens and the earth will obey his Messiah, (the sea and all th)at is in them. He will not turn aside from the commandment of the Holy Ones.

In order to maintain parallel thought, Cook says, the plural is required in the second line as in the first:

> Heaven and earth will obey his anointed ones,
> Nothing in them will turn aside from the commandment of the holy ones.

In a footnote, Cook states that "the sea and all...," proposed by Wise and Tabor to restore the text, cannot fit the available space. To bolster his case, Cook points to an "unambiguous" plural in "another fragment from the same scroll."

Although he considers other possibilities-anointed ones might be priest-representatives of Israel - the plural "Messiahs" could also be the Messiahs of Aaron and Israel. Because they are described in such exalted terms (heaven and earth will obey them), I consider it likely that the reference here is simply to two Messiahs.

Before we leave this topic it is well to mention that identification of Melchizedek with the Messiah, a feature of Hebrews, is found in another Qumran Scroll, 11QMelch. In fact, Buchanan calls it "the most important pre-Christian identification of Melchizedek with the Messiah."[57]

In 11QMelch, Melchizedek was expected to proclaim release to certain captives, ("sons of light") and "atonement for their sins." The author of this scroll identified Melchizedek as the Messiah, using terminology found in Hebrews: Son and High Priest.[58]

Even if the two Messianic functions - that of Priest and King - were coalesced into one person, in some documents, they remain distinctive characteristics of the Messiah. A Priest-Messiah, not a normative expectation outside Qumran, but important to the Sect, finds ample delineation in the Epistle to the Hebrews.

Undeniably, Melchizedek had an exalted status at Qumran, and scholars have argued that the writer of Hebrews was well aware of this fact.[59] However, the centrality of priesthood in the epistle is developed far beyond the fragmentary text of 11QMelch.

A priestly Messiah, one who is High Priest, is a theme given primacy in Hebrews (Ch. 4:14-10:14). The central concept of Jesus as High Priest is original to Hebrews. Jesus as High Priest is "the great thesis of the epistle ... almost unique in the New Testament ... Paul hints at the thought ... (Rom. 8:34b), but he does not develop the idea."[60]

In summary, the author argues for a single Messiah who combines identities of King and Priest. Melchizedek is presented, exalted and eternal, a foreshadowing of Christ. Finally, Jesus is delineated as High Priest. In each case, the author of Hebrews has engaged his readers in dialogue with Essene concerns.

Where are the former Essenes who are addressed so convincingly? They are gathered into a church with common experiences. In a place where many Essenes had once come, and where other Jews were influenced by their beliefs. Where is their church? We return now to the Fact-Comparison Chart.

The Mode of Conversion

We know how the author was converted, for we are told the circumstances. Certain people reiterated the word of salvation they once heard from Jesus. The same is true of recipients of the letter (Heb. 2:3). This is a choice clue to their location and circumstances.

For example, in Jerusalem the church was made up largely of men and women who heard Jesus teach. Would anyone describe them as converts of men who heard Jesus teach - a claim they could make for themselves?[61] Unlikely.

Apostles and other Palestinian disciples compassed Asia and southern Europe. Only Corinth fails to fit the profile as a city where conversion by eye witnesses was typical. We know the church in Rome was founded by such persons. William Barclay is on the right track when he says City X was visited by apostles, although its church was not directly founded by them.[62] The author was in City X in the early days and must have been one of the founders. I name Timothy and Paul, with whom the author was closely associated, as two other founders (Heb. 13:23). From the chart, you can see we may be talking about Ephesus.

Who were the apostolic preachers in Ephesus, who had seen and heard Jesus? First, John the Apostle. From 37 to 48 A.D. there is no direct word of his whereabouts, but many scholars place him in Ephesus and no one seriously challenges them.[63] The affinity of his gospel with Qumran is one reason to go along with his presence at the Essene colony of Ephesus. Eusebius cites Origen (ca. 225 A.D.) to the effect that John's sphere of action was Asia.[64] Irenaeus (2nd century) names John as a teacher in Ephesus, and Paul the founder of its church.[65] Many sources locate John in Ephesus in his later years, paying tribute to his enormous influence in Asia[66] where he died.[67]

Another disciple of Jesus, by the same name, was John the Presbyter or Elder, whom Papias (1st century) distinguished from the apostle.[68] Eusebius believes a second tomb inscribed "John," in Ephesus, was for this other eminent leader. Some scholars associate him with the Book of Revelation, whose author calls himself a prophet, not an apostle (Rev. 22:9). Other eyewitnesses in Ephesus were refugees from Palestine whom we cannot name.

Glancing across the third section of the chart we come to Alexandria. We know Christianity came to Alexandria, but how and when and by whom is obscure.[69] Jerome traces it to Mark.[70] As the tradition goes, Mark was the first man to preach the gospel and found a church in Egypt.[71] Not everyone agrees. Carrington thinks it is only a legend.[72] Wikenhauser even doubts if Mark was the first Bishop of Alexandria - as Eusebius was first to record.[73]

Did an apostle, namely Mark, preach in Alexandria? If so, an eyewitness brought the word of salvation. But the city is in no way enabled to match City X by this tradition, even if it were reliable. Why? Because even the tradition dates Mark's visit to Egypt after the death of Peter and Paul (ca. 67 A.D.).[74] We can pretty well account for Mark between Pentecost and 67 A.D., and Egypt was not in his itinerary.[75] Then who was the eyewitness who preached in City X if X = Alexandria? We simply don't know. Ephesus fits the equation much better.

Organization and Leadership

Scanning the fourth section of the chart, we see Rome had strong leadership. But if we try to equate its church organization with that of X we have nothing to go on. By contrast, we know much more about the organization and leadership of the

Ephesian church in 65 A.D. or so. Its resemblance to Church X is nothing less than remarkable.

Paul, Priscilla, Aquila, Timothy and Erastus were early evangelists, building on the foundation of apostles. Paul moved on, leaving Priscilla and Aquila. Timothy and Erastus left at the same time. Eventually Timothy was re-assigned to Ephesus. Of the native leaders, we know several by name. Tychicus (from Asia) and Trophimus (an Ephesian) were Paul's aides. Later we hear of Onesiphorous, an Ephesian loyal to Paul. Parenthetically, Apollos' territory was Corinth, and his stay in Ephesus was brief (Acts, Ch. 18, 19).

Who took over when Paul left? A well-trained native ministry - elders of the church (Acts, Ch. 20). They were charismatic office-holders, for the Holy Spirit had made them guardians of the church. "Take heed to yourselves and to all the flock..." Paul told them, and departed.

Now read the description of Church X. Bowman takes note of two sets of leaders in Hebrews; the early group of founders (Heb. 13:7) who are no longer there, and the permanent leaders who are "keeping watch over your souls"[76] (Heb. 13:17).

Quality of leadership in both churches is another point of identity. The affection of the Ephesian elders for Paul and their dedication to their calling is portrayed in Acts (Ch. 20). How like the leaders of Church X, who knew Timothy, Paul's associate, and diligently guarded their "flock."

Spiritual Condition

Even more ineluctable is the amazing similarity in the spiritual condition of the two churches, X and Ephesus.

At first, the word of eyewitnesses was bolstered by acts of God who "...also bore witness by signs and wonders and various miracles..." So wrote the author of Hebrews (Heb. 2:4), maybe with John the Apostle in mind, who by the power of God restored life to a dead man at Ephesus. Apollonius, writing ca. 225 A.D., recorded the incident.[77] Other signs and wonders came through Paul who healed the sick and cast out evil spirits (Acts 19:1,12,16,17). So far as we know, Ephesus is the only city where many were converted by Paul's miraculous gifts.

We are sure Hebrews was designed to spur the flagging zeal of the readers. They are warned against apathy (Heb. 12:12,13) and faintheartedness (Heb. 12:3). "How shall we escape if we neglect such a great salvation?" (Heb. 2:3a). "Not neglecting to meet together, as is the habit of some" (Heb. 10:25). Their apathy is set against a background of former faith, for which they suffered cheerfully (Heb. 10:32-34). Just like the church at Ephesus, where religion had lost, in some measure, the exaltation of the Holy Spirit but the doing of good deeds remained. The Church addressed in Hebrews was noted for charitableness, a virtue that is commended (Heb. 6:10). So was the church at Ephesus. (A trait excluding Jerusalem, a center of poverty, needing the ministration of other churches.)

Conditions at Ephesus are spelled out plainly in the message of John in the Book of Revelation (Rev. 2:2-4):

> I know your works, your toil and your patient endurance,...but you have abandoned the love you had at first...

Like the church in Hebrews, Ephesian Christians had to be reminded to meet for Holy Communion and prayer. Ignatius' Epistle to the Ephesians urged them to do so more often.[78]

Unhappily, false teachers arose from ecclesiastical ranks in Ephesus. Paul's prediction was fulfilled:

> I know that after my departure fierce wolves will come in among you, not sparing the flock; and from among your own selves will arise men speaking perverse things, to draw away the disciples after them. Therefore be alert...
>
> (Acts 20:29-31a).

Years later, John cited men who call themselves apostles but are not (Rev. 2:2). With deep concern for the church, Paul urged Timothy to stay in Ephesus to combat purveyors of false doctrine (I Tim. 1:3). Paul delineates their particular views with a few bold strokes. Fruitless speculation about myths, genealogies, and Law engaged their attention. All this was diversionary to Christians, who should trust God and walk according to the Spirit (I Tim. 1:4-11). To make matters worse, a fringe group - the Nicolaitans (Rev. 2:6) - were promoting immorality, and the eating of food sacrificed to idols (Rev. 2:14,15). Nicolaitans were a sect in the churches of Ephesus and nearby Pergamum.[79] Their doctrine was that of Balaam,[80] and they were quite a problem. John rebukes them (Rev. 2:6,14,15); so do Peter (II Peter 2:15) and Jude (Jude 7-11).

Beset by false teachings, Ephesus held its own against the onslaught, rejecting would-be apostles, and the works of the Nicolaitans (Rev. 2:2,6).

How do these facts match specific problems in the letter to the Hebrews? Perfectly. The threat of reversion to Judaism was of major proportions, judging by the author's careful attention to it. The "New Morality" of the Nicolaitans comes in for brief but crushing censure (Heb. 12:15-17).

THE DATE OF REVELATION

Is the Book of Revelation, to which we referred, a valid source of information for the Church at Ephesus in 65 A.D.? Yes, even when scholars date it 90-96 A.D., in the reign of Domitian. Major trends in the church can run 25 to 30 years or longer.

A viable alternative to the traditional date is 64-68 A.D., in the reign of Nero or 68-69 A.D., shortly after his death. Many exegetes have argued for it.[81] John could have been banished in the severe persecution instigated by Nero.[82] The Muratorian Canon (lines 48-50) implied the earlier date, saying Paul wrote to only seven churches "following the rule of his predecessor".[83] John, as we know, wrote Revelation to seven churches. Obviously, if Revelation preceded Paul's death, an early date is required.

At least part of Revelation was written before 70 A.D., for it incorporates early apocalyptic material. And the prophecy that both the Temple and the city of Jerusalem would be preserved (Rev. 11:1,2) is not the kind of prediction one would immortalize after both were destroyed.

For these reasons the evidence of John's Revelation is admissible in court.

Persecution Encountered by Christians

Another road sign pointing to Ephesus is the type of persecution met by the readers in City X. They were mocked and robbed. Some may have been imprisoned (Heb. 10:32-34). Despite their severe suffering they had not yet shed their blood (Heb. 12:4).

Ephesus fits much better than Rome where the Neronian persecution erupted in 64 A.D. after many years of continual jeopardy. As for Jerusalem - Christians there had died for their faith. Stephen's martyrdom by stoning was followed by harassment and imprisonment of disciples. James, the brother of John, was beheaded. James the Righteous was thrown from a parapet and beaten to death in 62 A.D.,[84] about three years before the writing of Hebrews. The date of his death is attested by Josephus and the second-century Christian historian Hegesippus.[85]

We surmise the persecution at Ephesus was not unto death. Ephesus had the highest ratio of converts to total population of any city in the world. In the first century Asia Minor was "the spiritual centre of Christianity," where the new faith spread most rapidly.[86] A marked contrast to Rome, where marytrdom was common and the growth of the church much slower. Tacitus' "immense multitude" of believers in 64 A.D.[87] were only a few thousand at most.[88] Here are some statistics to show how the threat of death kept down the number of Christians in Rome:

Date	*Estimated Christians in Rome*
65 A.D.	a few thousand[89]
ca. 200 A.D.	10,000[90]
250 A.D.	40-50,000 in the reign of Decius[91] (Gibbon estimates 50,000)
300 A.D.	70-80,000 at most at the time of the Diocletian persecution[92] (Harnack estimates 60-120,000 at the beginning of the 4th century)[93]

The faster growth of Christianity in Ephesus was the result of milder conditions, that posed no imminent threat to the lives of believers.

When did the people of Church X endure sufferings? Right after they were "enlightened" (Heb. 10:32), or baptized. Barclay notes the verb "to be enlightened" (photizesthai) became a synonym for "to be baptized."[94] And when did the Christian of Ephesus endure sufferings? We know a riot was instigated against Christians in the vast amphitheatre of the city when the church was being founded and Paul was still there (Acts, ch. 19). In other words, *soon after many were baptized.*

The jeering mob seized Gaius and Aristarchus, Paul's aides (Acts 19:29). Who can doubt that in the riotous atmosphere of the city, Christians were subject to mockery in Ephesus, as in City X? Ominously, Carrington notes the theatre held over 20,000 people. That it was filled by rioting non-Jews is proof of ugly anti-Christian sentiment in the city.[95] Christianity posed a threat to the craftsmen who sold souvenir replicas of the Temple of Artemis. Another sign of the swift success of the new faith, but it meant trouble for its followers.

In City X their property was plundered (Heb. 10:34). Is there any evidence that this happened to the Christians of Ephesus? Indeed there is. Melito, bishop of Sardis in Asia in the second century, petitioned Emperor Antoninus for redress of grievances. Plundering of Christians' property, which took place sporadically in Asia, had become an everyday occurrence:

> What never happened before is happening now - religious people as a body are being harried and persecuted by new edicts all over Asia. Shameless informers out to fill their own pockets are taking advantage of the decrees to pillage openly, plundering inoffensive citizens night and day... (From "Petition to Antoninus").[96]

Christians were being blackmailed by a disapproving populace egged on by official decrees. It started in the reign of Nero:

> ...Of all the emperors, the only ones ever persuaded by malicious advisers to misrepresent our doctrine were Nero and Domitian, who are against the Christians...[97]

Nero began to rule in 54 A.D., soon after Priscilla came to Ephesus and the church there was being founded. Believers began to be troubled by the plundering of their property not long after they were baptized. They lived in Asia. Those who lived in the city of Ephesus were harassed for undermining the Artemis cult, and the loss of profit they caused the craftsmen.

Another piece of the puzzle fits into place: In Heb. 10:34 the congregation is commended because they "had compassion on the prisoners..." Who were the prisoners? Were they Christians imprisoned for their faith, or prisoners in general? From the context, we sense that perhaps none of the author's own people were imprisoned, but they came to the aid of those who were. Now, Ramsay informs us that Ephesus was the seaport at the end of a road. Prisoners destined for Rome were led along this road. They came from all parts of the province of Asia.[98] Some were criminals. Some were on their way to be martyrs for Christ. They were marched along the road and then through the streets of the city.

In their ranks was Ignatius of Antioch, who was martyred about 110 A.D. Ignatius was under strict military guard as he passed through Asia on his way to Rome. But he preached to Christians in every city along the way.[99] To the church at Ephesus he wrote: "Ye are a high road of them that are on their way to die unto God."[100]

From this we see the Christians of Ephesus were singularly situated to "have compassion on the prisoners," of whom many were believers in chains.

If we posit that the author's city was Ephesus we explain the reference in Hebrews to what appears to be a special ministry to prisoners. Another match with City X.

Having studied the Fact-Comparison Chart, let's solve for X.

X DOES NOT EQUAL "JERUSALEM"

The Fact-Comparison Chart fails to equate Jerusalem with City X. The spiritual status of its church, its poverty, the martyrdoms that occurred there, are different. The allusion to eyewitnesses is illogical, if directed to a place where everyone can make the same claim. Erdman wraps up the case against Palestine in general by noting that Hebrews was not written in Aramaic - the language of the people. Not much use writing a letter in Greek to people whose knowledge of the language is marginal at best.

X DOES NOT EQUAL "ALEXANDRIA"

"Unknown" is the best word to describe the church at Alexandria in 65 A.D. Carrington remarks on the deficiency of evidence about Alexandrian Christianity, an area unrelated to any New Testament book.[101] If Mark evangelized there, he started after the deaths of Peter and Paul in 67 A.D. We may safely infer that the church was founded relatively late. Obviously, there was no time for the church to be founded, to endure trials, to practice charitableness, and to drift into spiritual languor, when Hebrews was written.

Still, a school persists naming Alexandria the destination of the Epistle. Daniélou links Hebrews to Egypt, where Essenism was entrenched.[102] His reason, which is a good one, can be applied to Ephesus with equal validity. Again and again I read that Philo's influence on Hebrews needs an Alexandrian locale. His use of allegory to explain scripture and his fondness for the word "Logos"[103] are thought to underlie much of Hebrews. However, where Philo's ideas and vocabulary occur in

Hebrews, they are adapted to Christian outlook by the author. Then too, Philo in turn was influenced by Essenes, whom he greatly admired, and their literature. We have talked in detail about Essenes, who numbered about 4000,[104] and found they were by no means confined to Alexandria. Let it suffice to say that Priscilla was acquainted with Philo and his writings.

A credibility gap confronts us in Alexandria. In the second century, eminent church scholars in that city collected and edited early New Testament texts. Among them were Origen and Clement of Alexandria, who had a role in recovering original manuscripts.[105] It was there tradition affirmed the Pauline authorship of Hebrews.[106] Peake is sure that if Hebrews were sent to Alexandria, the city's brilliant scholars, with all their exhaustive studies, would know Paul did not write it.[107] Needless to add, if Apollos were the author his native city would be aware of the fact in the first and second centuries and proud to proclaim it.

X DOES NOT EQUAL "ANTIOCH"

Syrian Antioch was an important city in the Roman Empire. A sanctuary from persecution in Palestine, this is where followers of Jesus were first called Christians, and where foreign missions originated. Unlike the church described in Hebrews, Antioch was a thriving evangelistic center, where the break with Jewish law was supported (Gal. 2:11).

X DOES NOT EQUAL "CORINTH"

The predominantly Gentile church at Corinth is a poor match for City X. Whatever its faults and difficulties, the church in that city had not drifted into spiritual apathy. Contrariwise, an abundance of spiritual gifts prevailed, leading at times to factionalism. Lacking strong, native leadership, the church looked to outside help in settling disputes.

"X DOES NOT EQUAL ROME"

Many scholars have favored Rome as the destination of the letter. Harnack was in their ranks; the dialogue with Essenism in the letter, of course, would not have been known to him.

A glance at the Fact-Comparison Chart reveals that Roman demographics comprised many Jews; however, the city was not, like Ephesus, a large Essene enclave. The Church, which was predominantly Gentile, had many former proselytes to Judaism. For these Gentile Christians and former proselytes, the Messianic identity of Jesus was not a compelling issue. Even for Jewish Christians, who were not former Essenes, faith did not hinge on this concept.[108] Indeed, Jesus as Messiah is conspicuously absent from Paul's Epistle to the Romans.

By contrast, Jesus as Messiah is central to the Epistle to the Hebrews. Why would anyone write so fervently to the Hebrew Christians of Rome in the context of Jewish-Essene beliefs, knowing that most of these people were not former Essenes? Or chide the Christians of Rome, renowned for their faith (Rom. 1:8), for spiritual languor? Or say they had not yet shed their blood, when persecution and martyrdom had been their lot?

Lee Anna Starr, writing in 1926, concurs with Harnack in placing Hebrews along the Rome/Ephesus axis, but has the letter written at Rome. She compares Heb. 5:11,12 with Rom. 15:14, and finds a crucial disparity. In the first case, the recipients are "dull of hearing" and ought to be teachers by now, considering the time invested in them; in the latter case, the recipients are filled with knowledge and well able to admonish (that is, teach) one another. Starr deems it obvious that that the two epistles were addressed to different cities.[109]

No, X $\neq$ Rome.

Nonetheless, Hebrews was known and valued at Rome; the author was esteemed in that city; and copies were circulated from there. Without changing the equation, all this is suggestive of the *city of origin.* Accordingly, our next stakeout will be in Rome.

X EQUALS EPHESUS

Meanwhile, our stakeout in Ephesus has proven productive. All we know about the author's church matches what we know about Ephesus: its people, its concerns, its spiritual history. We are not plagued by conflicting leads, nor puzzled by missing data. So copious is the evidence, so irrevocably does it lead to one city, we are no longer in doubt. The destination of Hebrews was Ephesus. A fact limiting its authorship to leaders in the Ephesian church. As the field narrows, the case for Priscilla continues its momentum.

NOTES TO CHAPTER VII

1. Wikenhauser, *op. cit.*, p. 466,467.
2. Millar Burrows, *The Dead Sea Scrolls* (New York: The Viking Press, 1955, reprinted by Gramercy Publishing Co., NY by arrangement with Viking Penguin, 1986), p. 329.
3. Ephesians, I and II Corinthians, and Timothy to his disciples at Ephesus. Raymond E. Brown, "The Qumran Scrolls and the Johannine Gospel and Epistles," *The Scrolls and the New Testament*. ed. Krister Stendahl. (New York: Harper & Bros., Publishers, 1957), p. 290, note 117.
4. Paul addressed Gentile converts in his Epistle to the Ephesians, which is a circular letter to various Asian communities (Wikenhauser, p. 423ff). I will not discuss Ephesians, as it yields no relevant information.
5. Wikenhauser, p. 463.
6. In 1884 H. von Soden detailed this view. Juelicher, Harnack, Wrede, F. Barth, A. Seeberg, Windisch, Michaelis, Oepke, Moffat, E. F. Scott, Dubarle, Schierse and Wikenhauser (writing in 1956) concurred. *Ibid.*
7. Kosmala made this discovery in "Hebraer, Essener, Christen" (Leiden, 1959). He presents the most comprehensive discussion of the relationships. Barth, *op. cit.*, p. 265, note 11.
8. According to Braun. See Raymond E. Brown, *op. cit.*, p. 290, note 111.
9. *Ibid.* See C. Spicq, "L'Epitre aux Hebreux," Vol. I, p. 109-138.
10. John Wick Bowman, *The Letter to the Hebrews, The Layman's Bible Commentary*, Vol. 24 (Richmond: John Knox Press, 1962), p. 12.
11. Daniélou, *op. cit.*, p. 112.
12. Edward M. Cook, *Solving the Mysteries of the Dead Sea Scrolls* (Grand Rapids, Michigan: Zondervan Publishing House, 1994), p. 86.
13. *Ibid.*, p. 88.
14. James C. Vanderkam, "Implications for the History of Judaism and Christianity," *The Dead Sea Scrolls After Forty Years* (Wash., DC: Biblical Archaeology Society, Symposium at the Smithsonian Institution Oct. 27, 1990, c. 1991, 1992), p. 21,26.
15. Bowman, *op. cit.*, p. 13 and Allegro, *op. cit.*, p. 101.
16. Bowman, p. 13. I find these allusions in Heb. 7:22; 8:6, 7, 8, 9, 10, 13; 9:15; 10:9, 16, 20, 29; 12:24 and 13:20.
17. Burrows, *op. cit.*, p. 337.

18. *Ibid.*, p. 371.

19. *Ibid.*, p. 365.

20. Burrows, p. 385.

21. Bowman, *op. cit.*, p. 14,15.

22. *Peloubet's Bible Dictionary*, ed. F. N. Peloubet and Alice D. Adams (Phil.: Universal Book and Bible House, c. 1947 by The John C. Winston Co. in Great Britain), p. 59. See Lev. Ch. 16.

23. Bowman, p. 14,15.

24. H. Brownlee, "John the Baptist in the New Light of Ancient Scrolls," *The Scrolls and the New Testament*, p. 37.

25. Brownlee, *op. cit.*, p. 37.

26. *Ibid.*, p. 38.

27. Burrows, p. 374, 375.

28. *Ibid.*, p. 363.

29. *Ibid.*, p. 350.

30. *Ibid.*, p. 261.

31. *Ibid.* See Thanksgiving Psalm VI (iii. 19-36), Burrows, p. 404, 407.

32. Burrows, p. 337.

33. Allegro, *op. cit.*, p. 132.

34. *Ibid.*

35. Burrows, p. 374.

36. Allegro, p. 132.

37. *Ibid.*

38. Burrows, p. 374.

39. Bowman, p. 12.

40. *Peake's Commentary on the Bible*, p. 859.

41. Daniélou, *op. cit.*, p. 94.

42. Karl Georg Kuhn, "The Two Messiahs of Aaron and Israel," *The Scrolls and the New Testament*, p. 64 and Vanderkam, *op. cit.*, p. 36.

43. Burrows, p. 264, 265.

44. *The Holy Bible, New Encyclopedic Reference Edition,* p. 1118. See also Burrows, p. 264, 265 and Daniélou, p. 113.

45. The Manual of Discipline (Qumran Document 1QS ix) and the Two-Column Document (1QSa ii, 12-17), Kuhn, *op. cit.*, p. 55. See also Shemaryahu Talmon, "Waiting for the Messiah: The Spiritual Universe of the Qumran Covenanters," *Judaisms and Their Messiahs at the Turn of the Christian Era* (Cambridge: Cambridge University Press, 1987), p. 122,123.

46. *Ibid.*

47. Allegro, p. 151,152.

48. *Ibid.*

49. *Ibid.*, p. 154.

50. Bowman, p. 14.

51. Daniélou, p. 113 and Allegro, p. 153, 154.

52. *The Holy Bible, New Encyclopedic Reference Edition*, p. 1118.

53. *Peake's Commentary on the Bible*, p. 578.

54. Bowman, p. 14.

55. Michael O. Wise and James D. Tabor, "The Messiah at Qumran," *Biblical Archaeology Review* Vol. 18 No 6, Nov/Dec 1992, 60-65.

56. Cook, *op. cit.*, p. 166,167. Taken from the book, *Solving the Mysteries of the Dead Sea Scrolls* by Edward M. Cook. Copyright © 1994 by Edward M. Cook. Used by permission of Zondervan Publishing House.

57. Buchanan, *op. cit.*, p. 99. See Attridge., *op. cit.*, 192-194.

58. Buchanan, p. 99,100.

59. Lane, *Word Biblical Commentary* Vol. 47A, p. 161.

60. L. MacNeil, *The Christology of the Epistle to the Hebrews* (Chicago: Chicago University, 1914), p. 366.

61. Charles R. Erdman, *The Epistle to the Hebrews* (Phil.: The Westminster Press, 1934), p. 13.

62. William Barclay, *The Letter to the Hebrews (The Daily Study Bible)* (Phil.: The Westminster Press, 1955), p. xix.

63. Peter Bamm, *Early Sites of Christianity* tr., Stanley Godman (New York: Pantheon Books, 1957), p. 110,111.

64. Henri Daniel-Rops, *The Church of Apostles and Martyrs* (London: J. M. Dent & Sons, Ltd., and NY: E. P. Dutton & Co.,) p. 106.

65. Eusebius, p.128.

66. Daniel-Rops, *op. cit.*, p. 75; Wikenhauser, p. 319 and *Peake's Commentary on the Bible*, p. 773.

67. Bamm, *op. cit.*, p. 261.

68. Eusebius, p. 150.

69. Daniel-Rops, p. 342.

70. *Ibid.*

71. Eusebius, p. 89.

72. Philip Carrington, *The Early Christian Church: Vol. I The First Christian Century* (NY: and London: The Syndics of the Cambridge Univ. Press, 1957), p. 313. Carrington adds that the Gospel of Mark seems to have been known in Egypt.

73. Wikenhauser, p. 163, citing Eusebius, (H.E. II 16.1).

74. *Peloubet's Bible Dictionary,* p. 386.

75. *Ibid.*, p. 385, 386.

76. Bowman, p. 90.

77. Eusebius, p. 225.

78. Ignatius probably wrote the epistle in the late first century. He died c. 110 A.D. *The Epistles of Rome and St. Ignatius of Antioch*, tr. James A. Kleist (Maryland: The Newman Bookshop, 1946), p. 65.

79. *Harper's Bible Dictionary*, p. 490.

80. *Peloubet's Bible Dictionary*, p. 449.

81. *Ibid.*, p. 556 and Wikenhauser, p. 554.

82. Wikenhauser, p. 54.

83. *Ibid.*

84. Eusebius, p. 72, quoting Clement of Alexandria.

85. Daniel-Rops, p. 45, 46 and Eusebius, p. 102.

86. According to Bishop Lightfoot. Ramsay, *The Church in the Roman Empire*, p. 171,172.

87. *Harper's Bible Dictionary*, p. 62.

88. Hertling, *op. cit.*, p. 6.

89. *Ibid.*

90. *Ibid.*, p. 22.

91. Maitland, *op. cit.*, p. 50.

92. Hertling, p. 6.

93. *Ibid.*, p. 197.

94. Barclay, *op. cit.*, p.56.

95. Carrington, *op. cit.*, p. 140.

96. Eusebius, p. 187.

97. *Ibid.*, p. 188.

98. Ramsay, *The Church in the Roman Empire*, p. 318, 319.

99. Eusebius, p. 145.

100. Ramsay, p. 318.

101. Carrington, p. 313.

102. Daniélou, p. 114.

103. Daniel-Rops, p. 288, 289.

104. "Essenes," *The Oxford Dictionary of the Christian Church*, Second Edition, ed. F. L. Cross and E. A. Livingstone. (New York: Oxford University Press, 1974, reprinted 1993), p. 471. Also Josephus, *Antiquities*, 18:21.

105. *Harper's Bible Dictionary,* p. 13.

106. Peake, *A Critical Introduction to the New Testament*, p. 73.

107. *Ibid.*

108. See George Macrae, S.J., "Messiah and Gospel," *Judaisms and Their Messiahs at the Turn of the Christian Era* (Cambridge: Cambridge University Press, 1987), p. 169-185.

109. Lee Anna Starr, *The Bible Status of Woman* (c. 1926 by Lee Anna Starr and reprinted in 1955 by Pillar of Fire, Zarephath, N.J.), p. 193, 194.

CHAPTER EIGHT

POSTMARK: ROME

If the Epistle to the Hebrews were put into an envelope, the address might be worded:

To the Hebrews
The Church at Ephesus
Ephesus, Province of Asia

The postmark would read:

ROME, ITALY
65 A.D.

Like Harnack, Professor Andrews and many of his colleagues have reasoned that Rome was the destination of Hebrews.[1] Let's review their arguments. In general, they give three reasons. First, Rome was like Church X, described in Hebrews, in charitableness, giving to Christians in need. That much is true, but as we have seen, the Christians of Rome, dying for their faith in the relentless persecution under Nero, cannot be the same people who had not yet shed their blood (Heb. 12:4). Even if the Epistle were dated before 64 A.D., when their ordeal started, we meet another objection. Church X had drifted into apathy, imperiling their souls. By contrast, the Roman church was an inspirational model of faith throughout the ancient world (Rom. 1:8; 16:19), as Paul wrote in 58 A.D.[2]

A second argument for Rome is that Hebrews was known there very early. Clement quoted from it freely in 96 A.D., showing that it was highly regarded. Here is a line of reasoning that can go in either direction. If the letter *originated* at

Rome, a copy remaining in the city, we have an equally good explanation for its early fame there.

A third argument for (destination) Rome, one that is often set forth, is found in the postscript. Signing off, the author wrote: "They of Italy salute you" (Heb. 13:24). The greeting is from Italian Christians, though the word "Christian" does not appear, nor is the word "brethren" used. Both words are clearly implied.

A specific geographical region is named. This can take us *to* or *from* Italy. Professor Andrews is not alone in his opinion that Hebrews was sent to Rome, with greetings from a group of expatriate Italians.[3] *If* he is right, "they of Italy" were in the same city as the author, somewhere outside of Italy.

Westcott thinks the phrase refers to Italians in a foreign land, admitting it could just as well mean Italians in Italy.[4] Since English translations vary, we should look at the Greek words:

οἱ ἀπὸ τῆς Ἰταλίας

They (who are) in Italy
from Italy
away from Italy

The preposition ἀπὸ is used in exactly the same way in another part of the New Testament:

οἱ ἀπὸ τῆς Θεσσαλονίκης

translated: "Those in Thessalonica" (Acts 17:13), referring in context to Jews of Thessalonica in their own city. Here is justification for translating Heb. 13:24, "They who are of (and in) Italy." Lane does not cite Acts 17:13; only Acts 18:2, referring to Priscilla and Aquila, expatriate in Corinth.[5] But Acts 18:2 isn't really comparable, since there the phrase is "having come from Italy," not "They of Italy."

Discoveries of ancient papyrus fragments and letters support the contention that "they of any city" refers to people in and not away from the city.

W. D. Gardiner, writing in *The Expositor* (1917), states the Greek word "ἀπὸ" meaning "of," or "from," or "away from," was practically equivalent to the preposition "en" or "in" throughout the papyrus discoveries. Census returns and tax receipts often used the terminology, "they of a certain city" (Oxyrynchus papyri # 171, 157, 158 etc.). The government wants to know *where its taxpayers are*, not where they are away from. There is no evidence in the papyri that the Palestinian mode of registration was prevalent through the Roman Empire. On the contrary, it is obvious that great care was taken to find out present residence since immediate notice of removal was required (Oxyrynchus papyri #251, 252, 253 etc.).

Gardiner asserts: "Our conclusion is that no inhabitant of the Mediterranean world of the first three centuries of our era, finding the Epistle to the Hebrews, and knowing no reason for taking its phrases in any special sense, would come to any other conclusion, after read chapter 13:24, than that the Epistle conveyed greetings from certain Christians resident in Italy."

Consider further, the translation "They who are away from Italy" creates a problem. Why should the author, writing to Rome (allegedly), send greetings only from expatriate Italian Christians, and not from all Christians in the city? Some scholars have tried to answer this objection by saying "They of Italy" are Jewish Christians expelled from Rome about 50 A.D., who regrouped in the author's city. But we know many Jews returned to Rome when Claudius died in 54 A.D. It is farfetched to have those who did not return remain with the author, then to have the author pass over all but this tiny fragment of the church in sending greetings.

There is intriguing information about the place of origin of Hebrews - to be weighed with other evidence. A subscript found in the early fifth century Codex Alexandrinus ("A") says the letter was "written from Rome." The sixth century Codex Euthalianus ("H") has "written from Italy," using the phrase "ἀρὸ τῆs Ἰταλίαs", showing that the phrase "was interpreted in certain circles as a greeting from within Italy."[6] Several other manuscripts have subscripts mentioning Rome, Italy, or in one case, Athens.[7]

"They of Italy" are most likely Christians in Italy. Italy, of course, denotes Rome, as it does in Acts 18:2. Only from Rome, a church center, would greetings logically be sent.

Date of Writing

Interwoven in our line of reasoning is the date of writing. We already know that Hebrews was written in apostolic times. The presence of men and women who had seen Jesus, and the author's firsthand knowledge of the incipient church (Heb. 10:32-34) need a date close to the primitive church. So do "signs and wonders" (Heb. 2:4). Only the first or second generation of believers will do.

Although suggested dates run the gamut from 58 to 110 A.D., an upper limit is set by Clement's use of the Epistle in 95 or 96. Timothy, the only living person mentioned by name, cannot be placed in the second century convincingly.

I agree with the consensus stamping the postmark 65-66 A.D.[8] Knowledgeable persons have long discerned what is obvious: Hebrews was designed to prevent apostasy. Jewish Christians were shown that the former covenant, filled with hope for the future, has come to fruition in the new. Ineffectual sacrifices of the priests have given way to the perfect, once-and-for-all sacrifice of Christ. Temple worship, with its inevitable imperfections, has culminated in worship mediated by the Savior. By reasonable deduction, the date must be prior to 70 A.D., when the Temple was demolished. Why else would the author fail to mention its destruction? And why else imply its continued operation (Heb. 10:11)?

When a fateful stone struck a pottery jar in a cave, in 1947, bringing new truth to light, we learned something more about the Epistle to the Hebrews. The Dead Sea Scrolls revealed a dialogue with Qumran doctrine, as we have detailed. Qumran was destroyed in 68-69 A.D.,[9] before the Temple fell. *By the same reasoning that dates the Epistle before 70 A.D. we now date it before 68-69 A.D.* Bowman moves the date back even further, to a period when the Qumran Sect was a viable rival to Christianity. That is, before the outbreak of the Jewish Roman War (66-70 A.D.).[10] Going along with Bowman, I posit a date prior to 66 A.D. for the writing of Hebrews.

Hebrews' striking resemblance to Stephen's speech in the seventh chapter of Acts leads many present-day scholars to date the Epistle fairly early. Stephen's sermon is clearly set in the context of Qumran, as mentioned before. For example, he cites an unusual text from the Old Testament book of Amos (Amos 5:26):

> And you took unto you the tabernacle of Moloch,
> and the star of your God Remphan.
>
> (Acts 7:43)

This text is used in the Damascus Document (VI, 14-15).[11] Daniélou thinks he refers to the Essene Teacher of Righteousness in Acts 7:52.[12] Also, Stephen quoted from the Samaritan text of the Pentateuch, a recension used by the Sect.[13]

See how Stephen and the author use the same arguments in the following chart, which is based on Bowman's analysis:[14]

HOW GOD REVEALS HIMSELF

According to Stephen (Acts 7:2-53)	***According to Hebrews***
1. God's revelation transcends national boundaries (Acts 7:2,9, 30-31, 36, 38)	1. Jesus is the universal savior who came "that by the grace of God he might taste death for every one" (Heb. 2:5-18)
2. God's revelation is independent of culture (Acts 7:17-22, 23-29)	2. Melchizedek, who was not a Jew, was a blessing to Abraham and his descendants (Heb. 7:4-10)
3. God's revelation is not bound to the Temple or the tabernacle (Acts 7:44-50)	3. Faith is independent of the city of Jerusalem (Heb. 11:10, 14-16, 23-31; 13:12-14)
4. God's revelation is not confined to the Jewish people, for they rejected His prophets (Acts 7:25-26; 35-36, 51-53)	4. Israel persecuted the prophets and rejected God's message (Heb. 3:17-19, Ch. 11)

From these identities we can logically assume, as many scholars do, that Hebrews is not far removed in time from Stephen's speech in the very first years of the church. Still, time had elapsed. A church had been founded in cities outside of Palestine. In the author's city, Christians had a second set of leaders. Their faith, enthusiastic at first, was faltering. At Ephesus the church was established in the early 50's. At least ten to fifteen years were needed for these conditions to hold true.

We are in Rome. The year is 65 A.D.

As time travellers, we continue our stakeout from a vantage point of safety. In our line of vision, however, there is danger for Christians, who were blamed by Nero for the fire of 64 A.D.

Why was Priscilla in Rome?

Thesis:	Priscilla wrote to the Hebrew Christians of Ephesus, from Rome, most likely in the year 65 A.D.
Question:	What was she doing in Rome in the midst of the Neronian persecution?
Mission:	To trace the events that led to the writing of the Epistle to the Hebrews.

Using whatever specific facts we have, let's attempt to reconstruct the circumstances. Now it's time to recall clues in the postscript:

- Timothy and the author are away from the locale of their ministry and plan to return as soon as they can.
- Timothy is in a place where his freedom has been limited by custody or imprisonment.
- The author, in the same location as Timothy or near by, is free to travel.

Please examine Paul's second letter to Timothy. In this elucidative document, Paul is in a Roman prison. A few years ago he was under house arrest but this time he is being treated severely. Writing to Timothy who is at Ephesus, he asks him to come to Rome as soon as he can (II Tim. 4:9), before winter if possible (II Tim. 4:21). "Bring Mark with you and the coat, books and parchments I left at Troas" (II Tim. 4 : 11-13), Paul asks. Remembering his friends Priscilla and Aquila who are with Timothy at Ephesus, he sends greetings to them (II Tim. 4:19). He conveys greetings from Pudens who is probably her relative (II Tim. 4:21). At last, the letter reaches Timothy, who reads it with deep concern. Then Priscilla and Aquila, who once risked their lives to save Paul, read the letter. They think of his suffering and peril. Timothy sets out for Rome. *Priscilla and Aquila go with him.*

Friendship was a decisive part of their decision to go. H. V. Morton portrays the affection of Paul for his two colleagues.[15] The trio had much in common: their Christian faith and - in the case of Aquila - Jewish background; and the trade of tentmaking in which they were coworkers. We mentioned Culver's hypothesis that Priscilla copied and circulated Paul's letters. Certainly, the author of Hebrews was familiar with Paul's writings, and most sympathetic to his teaching, though displaying great originality.[16]

This brings us to another matter requiring our attention and reasoning. Convergences between the writings of Paul and the Epistle to the Hebrews are exceptionally numerous, leading to speculation about a "literary relationship," (that is, one writer was copying another). One example, among many: Paul read Hebrews before writing I Corinthians, according to one scholar - or (more likely) Hebrews resounds with echoes of I Corinthians, according to others.[17] These similarities, in I Corinthians alone, range from doctrine (compare I Cor. 8:6 with Heb. 1:2) to imagery (compare I Cor. 9:24-28 with Heb. 12:1 and I Cor. 3:2 with Heb. 5:12) to the use of Old Testament scripture, especially Psalm 8, (compare I Cor. 15:27 with Heb. 2:6-9).

Why would a brilliant, independent thinker, such as the author of Hebrews, echo so many of Paul's ideas and even some of his imagery? Unless these ideas and images were hammered out together in many hours of conversation and companionship. Surely Priscilla, who extended hospitality to Paul in Corinth and possibly in Ephesus, had ample opportunity for long discussions with him.

Another bond existed between Priscilla and Paul, cementing their friendship based upon Christian faith. Just as Priscilla was from an illustrious family of Rome, Paul is thought to be from a leading family of Tarsus.[18] Paul's family had wealth and influence. His comparable social status made his friendship with Priscilla even more congenial.

Aristocratic status is a necessary inference from his Roman citizenship. The first settlement of Jews in Tarsus began in 171 B.C. To the oldest pioneer families, Antiochus gave citizenship.[19] Later Pompey, Julius Caesar, Antony and Augustus conferred citizenship upon persons of eminence, who were able to pay for it.[20] A special situation held at Tarsus, about 15 B.C.; Athenodorus deprived everyone of Tarsian citizenship who could not meet a property qualification.[21] Among those who remained on the roll, an inner circle held Roman citizenship as well. These distinguished families were the ruling aristocracy.[22]

Priscilla had a compelling reason to go to Rome. Her relative, Acilius Glabrio, was consul in 54 A.D.[23] Several other Acilians were senators or consuls in the first century. Consuls had the power to release prisoners and to free slaves.[24] If anyone could help Paul through high office or influence, Priscilla's family was likely to come to his aid. At any rate, she knew the ominous implications of his imprisonment. A fateful fire on July 19, 64 had led up to it,[25] nor was Paul alone in the "reprisals" that resulted from Nero's wrath. She wanted to see her friend who was close to martyrdom.

We can see Priscilla in her native city - visiting Paul prison, reunited with Pudens and her other relatives, saddened by the suffering of Roman Christians, yet mindful of her congregation in Ephesus where subtle danger lurked in the form of apathy and apostasy. We see her marshal her knowledge of scripture and her insight into the thinking of her people, admonishing them in stirring and elegant prose. She hinted at the fierce trials endured by Christians in Rome, by reminding Ephesians they had not yet had to die for their faith (Heb. 12:4).

Priscilla herself was free to go back, her aristocratic status having kept her out of prison, at least for now. Timothy had been taken into custody, but was about to be released and return to Ephesus (Heb. 13:23). He would become its first bishop, and end his days there.[26]

Priscilla and Aquila went back with him, but eventually returned to Rome. Paul and Peter were executed ca. 67 A.D., marking the end of their work for Christ in the world. Paul's friends survived him, but time was bringing their faith and labor to the same conclusion. One tradition places their martyrdom in Asia Minor, another in Rome, but we know they were buried in Rome.[27] The site of their burial is mentioned in all 7th century itineraries to the graves of Roman martyrs.[28]

But is Timothy Authentic?

Having alluded to Second Timothy, we are cognizant that the Pastoral Letters (Titus and I and II Timothy) have been under siege. Critics dispute their authenticity. Of the three letters, II Timothy is the least disputed, and all critics find genuine Pauline notes and paragraphs in it.[29] Personal references abound in the first and fourth chapters of Paul's second letter to Timothy. They ring true as genuine words of Paul. Barclay accepts all of II Timothy, chapter 4 on the ground that only Paul could have written it.[30]

Walter Lock thinks there are two, maybe three, letters combined in II Timothy. He discerns a general letter written from Rome during a second imprisonment, and a private letter (II Tim. 4:9-2).[31] The private letter, says Lock, is from either Paul's first imprisonment (Acts ch. 28) *or* the second, about 64 A.D.[32]

Why did Lock weigh the possibility of the earlier date? Paul's ambiguous remark about a first defense and his “rescue from the lion's mouth”[33] made Lock think he was writing at the end of his house arrest in Rome. Lock's view is unnecessary. At least one commentator thinks Paul was merely recalling an earlier incident, expressing hope for a “similar deliverance” despite his grim circumstances.[34]

Paul must have been writing during a second imprisonment. Certain facts do not fit the earlier date:

(1) A quick look at Acts, ch. 28 finds Paul in his own dwelling, with a guard, preaching and teaching the Word to scores of persons freely and contentedly. That the was the nature of the *first* imprisonment. In II Tim. 4:11, only Luke is with him, and Paul is depressed.

(2) Another look at Acts (20:5, 6) informs us that Paul last visited Troas about five years before his first imprisonment in Rome, as Wikenhauser brings out. So if II Tim. 4:13 was written then, Paul's coat and books were in Carpus' house five years![35] If Paul was released, and later visited Troas again, as tradition states, then his request to Timothy came in the second imprisonment.

(3) Now take a third look at Acts (21:29). Trophimus is with Paul in Jerusalem. But in II Tim. 4:20, Paul left him sick at Miletus![36] Obviously, we must date the fourth chapter of II Timothy - all of it - in Paul's later imprisonment, about 64 or 65 A.D. His letter to Timothy reached Ephesus just at the right time to cause Priscilla's presence in Rome about the year 65. Having means, motive, and opportunity, there she wrote the Epistle to the Hebrews.

This is the scenario.

Before ending our stakeout in Rome, one more foray into scripture.

A note is sounded in Hebrews, resonant with longing for a distant land. In chapter eleven, Abraham sets out in faith and arrives at an interim destination, only to live "as in a foreign country." The theme is extended to include his innumerable descendants, "strangers and foreigners on the earth...," seeking a homeland that will never be found on earth (Heb. 11:13-16). Their true home in heaven can only be seen and hailed from a distance.

Not they alone, but all believers, endure a haunting sense of alienation while on earth. "For here we have no lasting city," and the city we seek can only be glimpsed from afar (Heb. 13:14).

Abraham's destiny was linked to geography, a specific location; in Hebrews, the promised land is transcendant, beyond our immediate reach. Is something more to be read in these lines - a wistful yearning for home, in the heart of an exile? Was the spiritualization of Abraham's quest for a city from a worldy to a heavenly realm, shaped in part by personal experience?

If so, the process is consistent with what we know about Priscilla. Driven from Rome by edict of Claudius, starting anew in the boisterous environment of Corinth, and again in Ephesus, even further afield, Priscilla had ample cause for homesickness.

In the New Testament, only Hebrews and I Peter 1-2 use sojourner imagery to describe the life of the Christian community.[37] In yet another instance, Hebrews is unique in all scripture.

Drawing from Greek literature, and likely from the experience of sea travel, the author depicts hope, that is, the hope we have in Christ, as an anchor of the soul (Heb. 6:19) In the ancient world, ships held fast by the anchor's teeth were the source of a metaphor for stability.[38]

An extended metaphor ensues, in which the anchor enters into a heavenly realm. Kenneth Wuest remarks on some rich imagery; the soul is a ship, storm-tossed on the sea of this present life. Faith secures the soul of the believer to that Divine refuge, hidden like the depths of the sea.[39]

Though common in literature, the anchor metaphor appears nowhere else in scripture. Attridge. notes that biblical Hebrew lacks a word for anchor. Where the word appears in the New Testament, it is not used symbolically (Acts 27:29, 30, 40)[40]

It is interesting to note that the anchor, as a Christian symbol, appears no less than sixty times in the Priscilla Catacomb.[41] Might one speculate that its unique inclusion in Hebrews had particular meaning for relatives and friends of Priscilla?

While the anchor metaphor is overtly nautical, other nautical imagery is "painted rather by suggesting than directly," according to James A. Robertson.[42] Words like "holding fast" or "drawing near" (like a ship approaching land); "drifting" (as from a course); being "swept about" (as in a current); "casting away" our confidence (as if it were ballast); "being on the outlook" and "seeing from afar" (as if to catch sight of the shore); all these indirect allusions are commonplace in the epistle.[43]

Two facts emerge from this discussion: the author is at home in the milieu of Greek literature, and has likely voyaged far from home. Transmuting a sense of estrangement and impermanence, this individual formulates an extended metaphor that reveals a poetic nature. Through indirection and allusion, other nautical images emerge. Our author is subtle, refined, and elegant. Yes, one might even say delicate and fastidious. While persons close to Paul, other than Priscilla, could conceivably meet these criteria, not many can meet all the other criteria and certain categories of persons are ruled out altogether.

We have completed our stakeout in Rome.

Final Summary and All Points Bulletin for Priscilla

In order to begin our investigation of the authorship of Hebrews we had to march past the siren song of Origen, "Who wrote Hebrews, God alone knows." We had to trudge through the valley of weary platitudes such as "Only Paul could have written it." We were haunted by ectoplasmic entities, "any one of whom could have written it."

To Origen, we say with Schiele that we have undertaken a fitting line of inquiry, in fact "we virtually have a list of names" in which the author appears, in the circle of Paul's friends.

To William Leonard, who strove valiantly amidst thinning ranks for Paul's authorship, we say "Your reasoning was tangential to the truth, for someone very close to Paul was the author."

At this time I want to call Leonard to the witness stand not as a witness for Paul, but as a surprise witness for Priscilla. This is his testimony, verbatim:

> "Then how could such a man be concealed, in the first ages of the church, when the memory of those who were very distinguished, has been preserved so distinct, and with so much care and reverence, by ecclesiastical tradition? Men, who can write in this manner, cannot remain concealed anywhere. And the writer of such an epistle, it would seem, must have acted a part not less conspicuous than that of the great apostle of the Gentiles himself."[44]

Well stated, and worthy to exorcise the specter of the hypothetical unknown person who "might have been the author." If I had a chance to cross-examine, I would ask two questions:

> First, don't you mean to say, "How could such a *person* be concealed" and "*Anyone* who can write in this manner, cannot remain concealed"?

> And second, "Has it ever occurred to you to ask w*hy* was such a person concealed"?

If it were possible I would call to the stand Clement of Rome, who made extensive use of the epistle to the Hebrews and never once alluded to the author. I would ask, "Were you really ignorant of the author's name? Or, as Arthur Peake implied, were you just not saying?"

We have come full circle to the starting point: Why was the name of the author lost?

The more we think about it, the stranger it becomes. Only one satisfactory answer can be proffered; the name was lost "accidentally on purpose" because Priscilla was the author.

In the search for an author we are virtually stumbling over Priscilla. No longer is it feasible to pretend she isn't there.

For example, if Martin Luther were on the witness stand, we might inquire: "If Apollos could have been the author, why couldn't Priscilla, his teacher, have been the author?"

In point of fact, whatever is true for Apollos - his learning, his preeminent leadership - goes double for Priscilla because the objections against Apollos do not apply to her.

Nevertheless, from Luther, naming Apollos in 1537 to Harnack, naming Priscilla in 1900, 363 years elapsed.

Inexplicably, from the writing of Hebrews in 65 to Harnack, 1835 years elapsed.

For a long time the world was in no mood to even consider the case for Priscilla. Harnack's hypothesis won a measure of support, but support was overshadowed by derision and eventual neglect. Schiele, Harris, Baker, Robertson, and Starr all gave cogent reasons for supporting Harnack, but Priscilla's claim to the authorship of Hebrews has not yet been vividly impressed upon the popular consciousness.

Today we are being challenged to weigh the evidence for Priscilla. Was she a close friend of Paul? Yes. Was she learned and cultured like her student Apollos? Yes. Did Apollos preach on the messiahship of Jesus, the main theme of Hebrews, following her instruction? Yes. Did she have a ministry in Ephesus, the destination of the letter? Yes. Did she have connections at Rome, where the letter was known, copied, and esteemed, and where the unique liturgy enshrines Melchizedek as high priest, as in the epistle? Yes.

Have we found example upon example of feminine outlook in the epistle? And example upon example of the inclusion of women among exemplars of faith? Yes.

Is there anyone else in Paul's circle, among outstanding leaders of the early church, who meets all these qualifications for authorship? We can take each person named in scripture, one by one, and show how one or more qualifications remain unmet. For one, the conversion story in Heb. 2:3 does not check out; another uses the Massoretic text instead of the Septuagint; another is commissioned an apostle to the Gentiles; another is inarticulate, lacking eloquence; another lacks refinement. Others we cannot visualize as caring about education and the parent-child relationship.

Now we come to the All Points Bulletin for the author of the hitherto anonymous Epistle to the Hebrews.

We have a description of the suspect, whose eminence, professionalism, and eloquent spirituality were a driving force in the evangelization of large population centers. We know *where* the author had a ministry (along the Rome/Ephesus axis, and in Corinth, the destination of another letter, in behalf of Apollos). We know with *whom* the author worked in close association - Paul and Timothy, and another individual, perhaps a spouse (judging from the alternation of pronouns "I" and "we"). We know the *content* of the author's teaching (the "doctrine of baptisms," (Heb. 6:2), and proof from scripture that Jesus was the Messiah). We know from Acts that Apollos, the student of Priscilla, was in need of instruction about baptisms, and we know that following her systematic teaching, he could forcefully proclaim Jesus to be the Messiah foretold in scripture. Thus Priscilla is doubly linked to the content of Hebrews.

Priscilla stands alone in the field of contenders. Priscilla - learned teacher of Apollos, dedicated leader of congregations, famous evangelist in the apostolic church, and with her husband Aquila, close companion of Paul.

She is our prime suspect, with means, motive and opportunity:

Means:	She had the requisite educational background.
Motive:	She was a spiritual leader temporarily separated from her flock, and concerned about their spiritual development.
Opportunity:	She had a ministry at Ephesus, the destination of the letter, and connections at Rome, the point of origin.

Priscilla, not Paul, whose blunt speech does not match the letter-writer's artistry and refinement very well.

Priscilla, not Apollos, whose eloquence and knowledge of scripture lend spurious credibility to his claim. Squared off against Paul, staking out territory that places him far from the scene, he could not be the mystery author of Hebrews.

Priscilla, not Barnabas, whose name would not have been lost, and who may have died before the letter was written.

Priscilla, not Philip the Deacon nor Zenas the lawyer, nor any other hapless "suspect" in the lineup, taken into custody by mistake, with faulty evidence, or caught in a dragnet inadvertently.

Priscilla, not a shadowy figure fleeing the limelight, with so little impact on the apostolic church as to elude any mention in scripture.

Priscilla, author of the Epistle to the Hebrews.

Charge to the Jury

Compelling evidence has been presented; ponder it well.

Together, we have delved into scripture, archaeology, and a wide variety of documents to glean the truth about an ancient mystery. Concomitant to knowledge is a mind that is open to truth.

Weigh the evidence, which is cumulative, and consider the line of reasoning in its entirety. Point by point the scale is tipped; Priscilla outbalancing the other candidates.

The scale tells us that the Epistle to the Hebrews should be ascribed to Priscilla.

Follow where the evidence leads, further along the path. This is about the apostolic church, and an eminent woman leader in that church. Therefore the path may lead to reconsideration of the apostolic age as a standard for today.

In those formative years, men and women pioneered a new faith. Gifts of the Holy Spirit, conferred without partiality, operating without hindrance, empowered the entire community.

That vision of our common humanity, transformed by grace, was the glory of the early church. May we descry the star that shone so brightly for them, as they stood on the threshold of a new spiritual era.

NOTES TO CHAPTER VIII

1. H. T. Andrews, "Hebrews," *The Abingdon Bible Commentary*, 1298.
2. Wikenhauser, p. 405.
3. Andrews, *op. cit.*, p. 1298
4. Westcott, *op. cit.*, p. xliii-xliv.
5. Lane, *Word Bible Commentary* Vol. 478, p. 571
6. Lane, p. 571; also Attridge., p. 410 and *Interpreter's Dictionary of the Bible* Vol. 2, p. 573.
7. Raymond E. Brown, Fitzmeyer, and Murphy, ed., *Jerome Biblical Commentary* (Englewood Cliffs, NJ: Prentice-Hall, Inc.,1968), 403 for mention of Athens.
8. Spence-Jones, *op. cit.*, p. 166.
9. Stendahl, *op. cit.*, p. 213.
10. Bowman, *op. cit.*, p. 15-16.
11. Daniélou, *op. cit.*, p. 95.
12. *Ibid.*
13. Allegro, *op. cit.*, p. 140.
14. Bowman, p. 11 .
15. Morton, *op. cit.*, p. 348, 349, 355, 380, 471.
16. Bowman, p. 10.
17. Hurst, *op. cit.*, p. 108-109; also Leonard, *op. cit.*, 160-168.
18. Morton, p. 9.
19. Ramsay, *Cities of St. Paul*, p. 184.
20. *Ibid.*, p. 195
21. *Ibid.*, p. 226.
22. *Ibid.*, p. 227.
23. *Real-Encyclopadie der Classischen Altertumswissenschaft*, Vol. I, p. 254. (See genealogical chart p. 115 this book.)
24. Poland, *op. cit.*, p. 299.
25. Spence-Jones, *op. cit.*, p. 25.

26. *The Columbia Encyclopedia,* 3rd edition, p. 2140 and *Harper's Bible Dictionary*, p. 762.

27. Coulson, *op. cit.*, p. 55; *The Catholic Encyclopedia*, Vol. 12, p. 428; and *The Book of Saints*, 5th ed., p. 78.

28. *The Catholic Encyclopedia*, Vol. 12, p. 428 citing De Rossi, *Roma Sotteranea*, I, 176,177.

29. *The Abingdon Bible Commentary*, p. 1274, 1275, 1285 and Ramsay, *The Bearing of Recent Discoveries on the Trustworthiness of the N.T.*, p. 414.

30. William Barclay, *The Letters to Timothy, Titus and Philemon.* (Phil.: The Westminster Press, 1961), p. 16.

31. Walter Lock, *A Critical and Exegetical Commentary on the Pastoral Epistles (I and II Timothy and Titus).* International Critical Commentary. (New York: Charles Scribner's Sons, 1924), xxxii-xxxiii.

32. *Ibid.*, p. 78.

33. II Tim. 4:16,17.

34. *The Abingdon Bible Commentary*, p. 1288.

35. Wikenhauser, p. 444.

36. *Ibid.*

37. Frank R. VanDevelder, *The Biblical Journey of Faith: The Road of the Sojourner* (Phil.: Fortress Press, 1988), p. 90.

38. Lane, *Word Biblical Commentary* Vol. 47A, p. 153.

39. Wuest, *op. cit.*, p. 125.

40. Attridge., p. 183.

41. R. Kent Hughes, *Hebrews: An Anchor for the Soul* Vol. I (Wheaton, IL: Crossway Books, 1993), p. 178.

42. Robertson, *op. cit.*, p. 159-160.

43. Some examples are: Heb. 2:1; 3:6,14; 4:14; 6:18; 7:19; 10:23, 35; 13:9.

44. Leonard, *op. cit.*, p. 171.

BIBLIOGRAPHY

BIBLES, LEXICONS, AND WORD STUDIES

The Holy Bible, Revised Standard Version. New York: Thomas Nelson & Sons, 1952.

The Holy Bible, New Revised Standard Version. Nashville: Thomas Nelson Publishers, 1989.

Schonfield, Hugh J., tr. *The Authentic New Testament.* New York: The New American Library of World Literature, Inc., 1958.

The Interlinear Greek-English New Testament. The Nestle Greek Text with a Literal English Translation by The Reverend Alfred Marshall and a marginal text of The Authorized Version of King James. Second edition. Grand Rapids: Zondervan Publishing House, 1959.

Sir Lancelot C. L. Brenton, tr. *The Septuagint with Apocrypha: Greek and English.* Peabody, MA: Hendrickson Publishers, 1990. Originally published by Samuel Bagster & Sons, Ltd., London, 1851.

Arndt, William F. and Gingrich, F. Wilbur, tr. *A Greek-English Lexicon of the New Testament and Other Early Christian Literature.* Chicago: The University of Chicago Press, 1957.

Ellingworth, Paul and Nida, Eugene A. *A Translator's Handbook on The Letter to the Hebrews.* London, New York, Stuttgart: United Bible Societies, 1983.

Moulton, James H. and Milligan, George. *The Vocabulary of the Greek New Testament.* Grand Rapids: Eerdmans, 1952.

Souter, Alexander, tr. *Novum Testamentum Graece.* Great Britain: Oxonii E. typographer Clarendoniano, 1910.

Vine, W. E. *New Testament Greek Grammar.* Grand Rapids: Zondervan Publishing House, 1965.

Wuest, Kenneth S. *Hebrews in the Greek New Testament.* Grand Rapids: Wm. B. Eerdmans Publishing Company, 1947.

BIBLE DICTIONARIES

Harper's Bible Dictionary. Madeleine S. Miller and J. Lane Miller. New York: Harper & Row, Publishers. 1st ed., 1952, 7th ed., 1961.

The Interpreter's Dictionary of the Bible. New York: Abingdon Press, 1962.

Peloubet's Bible Dictionary. ed F. N. Peloubet and Alice D. Adams. Phil.: Universal Book and Bible House, c. 1947 by The John C. Winston Co. in Great Britain.

COMMENTARIES

The Abingdon Bible Commentary. ed., Frederick Carl Eiselen, Edwin Lewis, and David G. Downey. New York: Abingdon-Cokesbury Press, 1929.

Attridge, Harold W., *The Epistle to the Hebrews: A Commentary on the Epistle to the Hebrews*. Helmut Koester, ed., *Hermeneia - A Critical and Historical Commentary on the Bible* Phil.: Fortress Press, 1989.

Barclay, William. *The Letter to the Hebrews*. (The Daily Study Bible) Phil.: The Westminster Press, 1961.

---, *The Letters to Timothy, Titus and Philemon*. Phil.: The Westminster Press, 1961.

Bowman, John Wick. "The Letter to the Hebrews", *The Layman's Bible Commentary*, Vol. 4. Richmond: John Knox Press, 1962.

A Commentary on the Holy Bible by various writers. ed., J. R. Dummelow. First printing, 1908. New York: The Macmillan Co., 1960, 24th printing.

Buchanan, George Wesley. *The Anchor Bible: To the Hebrews*. N.Y.: Doubleday, 1972.

Clarke, Adam. *Introduction to the Epistle of Paul the Apostle to the Hebrews*, 1810.

Dunn, James D. G. *Romans 9-16*. Word Biblical Commentary, Vol. 38. Dallas: Word Books, 1988.

Erdman, Charles R. *The Epistle to the Hebrews*. Phil.: The Westminster Press, 1934.

Matthew Henry's Commentary on the Whole Bible. Vol. VI, Acts to Revelation. New York: Fleming H. Revell Co., n.d.

L. D. Hurst, *The Epistle to the Hebrews: Its Background of Thought*. Cambridge, New York, Port Chester, Melbourne, Sydney: Cambridge University Press, 1990.

The Interpreter's Bible in Twelve Volumes. Vol. XI, "The Epistle to the Hebrews", introd. and exegesis by Alexander C. Purdy; exposition by J. Harry Cotton. New York and Nashville: Abingdon Press, 1955.

Jerome Biblical Commentary. Raymond E. Brown, Fitzmeyer, and Murphy, ed. Englewood Cliffs, NJ: Prentice-Hall, Inc., 1968.

Kittredge, Cynthia Briggs, "Hebrews," *Searching the Scriptures*,Vol. 2. New York: Crossroad, 1993-1994, p. 428-452.

Lane, William L. *Hebrews*. Word Biblical Commentary, Vol. 47A,B. Dallas: Word Books, Publisher, 1991.

Lock, Walter, *A Critical and Exegetical Commentary on the Pastoral Epistles (I and II Timothy and Titus)*. International Critical Commentary. New York: Charles Scribner's Sons, 1924.

Montefiore, Hugh. *A Commentary on the Epistle to the Hebrews*. New York: Harper & Row, Publishers, 1964.

Nairne, Alexander, ed. *The Epistle to the Hebrews with Introduction and Notes*. Cambridge: University Press, Cambridge, 1917, reprinted 1957.

The Expositor's Greek Testament. ed. W. Robertson Nicoll. Vol. IV, "The Epistle to the Hebrews" by Marcus Dods. London: Hodder & Stoughton Limited, n.d.

Peake's Commentary on the Bible. ed. Matthew Black. New Jersey: Thomas Nelson & Sons, Ltd., 1962.

Westcott, Brooke Foss. *The Epistle to the Hebrews: The Greek Text with notes and essays*. 1st ed., 1889, 2nd ed., 1892. Grand Rapids: Wm. B. Eerdmans Publishing Co. This edition is published by special arrangement with the Macmillan Co., 1955.

SOURCE BOOKS

Bettenson, Henry. ed. *Documents of the Christian Church*. New York: Oxford University Press, 1947.

Eusebius. *The History of the Church from Christ to Constantine*. tr., B. A. Williamson. Baltimore: Penguin Books, 1965.

Kleist, James A., tr. *The Epistles of Rome and St. Ignatius of Antioch*. Maryland: The Newman Bookshop, 1946.

Lightfoot, J. B., tr. and ed., completed by Harmer, J. R. "The Epistle of S. Clement to the Corinthians," *The Apostolic Fathers*. Grand Rapids: Baker Book House, 1970.

The Library of Christian Classics. General Editors John Baillie, John T. McNeill, Henry P. VanDusen. Vol. I *Early Church Fathers*. tr. and ed. Cyril C. Richardson, Eugene R. Fairweather and Edward Rochie Hardy. Philadelphia: The Westminster Press, 1953. Vol. XXI *Luther: Early*

Theological Works. ed. and tr., James Atkinson. Philadelphia: The Westminster Press and London: S. C. M. Press Ltd., 1962.

The Ante-Nicene Fathers, Vol. I. The Apostolic Fathers-Justin Martyr-Irenaeus. ed. Alexander Roberts and James Donaldson. (Grand Rapids: W. B. Eerdmans Publishing Co., 1950.)

St. Chrysostom, *Homilies on the Acts of the Apostles and The Epistle to the Romans, Nicene and Post-Nicene Fathers of the Christian Church*, Vol. XI. ed. Philip Schaff. New York: The Christian Literature Co., 1889.

F. L. Cross, ed., *Oxford Dictionary of the Christian Church*. First Edition, London: Oxford University Press, 1958. Second Edition, ed., F. L. Cross and E. A. Livingstone, 1974, reprinted 1993. Note: A reference to Peter the Deacon as Benedictine Abbey chronicler is in the First Edition.

C. D. Yonge, tr., *The Works of Philo Complete and Unabridged*. New Updated Editon, with Foreword by David M. Scholer. Peabody, Mass: Hendrickson Publishers, 1993.

NEW TESTAMENT STUDIES AND TIMES

Balsdon, J.P.V.D. *Roman Women: Their History and Habits*. New York: The John Day Co., 1963.

Bamm, Peter. *Early Sites of Christianity*. tr. Stanley Godman. New York: Pantheon Books, 1957.

Barth, Markus. "The Old Testament in Hebrews, an essay in Biblical Hermeneutics", *Current Issues in New Testament Interpretation: Essays in Honor of Otto A. Piper*. ed. Wm. Klassen and Graydon F. Snyder. New York: Harper & Bros., 1962.

Barton, Bruce. *The Book Nobody Knows*. Cutchogue, N.Y.: Buccaneer Books, 1992.

Barton, George A. *The Apostolic Age and the New Testament*. Philadelphia: University of Pennsylvania Press, 1936.

Bilezikian, Gilbert. *Beyond Sex Roles*, Second Edition. Grand Rapids: Baker Book House, 1985.

Burgon, John W. *The Last Twelve Verses of Mark*. The Sovereign Grace Book Club, 1959.

Carrington, Philip. *The Early Christian Church, Vol. I: The First Christian Century*. New York and London: The Syndics of the Cambridge University Press, 1957.

Chapman, John. "Aristion, Author of the Epistle to the Hebrews," *Revue Benedictine 22 (1905)*.

Comfort, Philip W. *Early Manuscripts and Modern Translations of the New Testament*. Wheaton: Tyndale House Publishers, 1990.

Culver, Elsie Thomas. *Women in the World of Religion*. New York: Doubleday & Co., 1967.

Cureton, William, tr. *Ancient Syriac Documents Relative to the Earliest Establishment of Christianity in Edessa and the Neighboring Countries*. Preface by W. Wright. Amsterdam: Oriental Press, 1967.

Daniel-Rops, Henri. *The Church of Apostles and Martyrs*. London: J. M. Dent & Sons, Ltd. and New York: E. P. Dutton & Co., 1960. tr. by Audrey Butler from L'Eglise des Apôtres et des Martyrs, 1948.

Davies, A. Powell. *The First Christian*. New York: Farrar, Straus & Cudahy, 1956.

Dozier, Verna J. and Adams, James R *Brothers and Sisters*. Boston: Cowley Publications, 1993.

Edmundson, George. *The Church in Rome in the First Century*. London: Longmans, 1913.

Ford, J. Massyngberde. "The Mother of Jesus and The Authorship of the Epistle to the Hebrews", *The Bible Today* 82 (1976).

Hanson, A. T. "Rahab the Harlot in Early Christian Tradition," *JSNT I (1978)*. (Journal for the Study of the New Testament).

Harnack, Adolph von, "Probabilia uber die Addresse und den Verfasser des Hebraerbriefes," *Zeitschift fur die Neutestamentliche Wissenschaft und die Kunde der aelteren Kirche*. E. Preuschen, Berlin: Forschungen und Fortschritte, 1900, Vol. I, 16-41.

-----*The Mission and Expansion of Christianity in the First Three Centuries*, Vol. 2. Second, enlarged and revised edition. Tr. and ed., James Moffatt. New York: G. P. Putnam's Sons and London: Williams and Norgate, 1908.

Harris, James Rendel. Lecture V, "Sidelights on the Authorship of the Epistle to the Hebrews," *Side-Lights on New Testament Research*. London: The Kingsgate Press, James Clarke & Co., 1908.

Hayes, D. A. *The Epistle to the Hebrews*, Biblical Introduction Series. New York, Cincinnati: The Methodist Book Concern.

Hughes, R. Kent. *Hebrews: An Anchor for the Soul* Vol. I. Wheaton, IL: Crossway Books, 1993.

Kip, Wm. Ingraham. *The Catacombs of Rome: as illustrating the church of the first three centuries*. New York: Daniel Dana, Jr., 1853.

Landers, Solomon. "Did Jephthah Kill His Daughter?" *Bible Review*, Aug., '91, Vol. VII No. 4.

Leonard, William. *The Authorship of the Epistle to the Hebrews: Critical Problem and Use of the Old Testament.* Rome, Vatican: Polyglot Press, 1939.

MacNeil, H. L. *The Christology of the Epistle to the Hebrews.* Chicago: Chicago University, 1914.

Maitland, Charles. *The Church in the Catacombs.* London: Longman, Brown, Green and Longmans, 1846.

Metzger, Bruce M. *The Text of the New Testament.* New York: Oxford University Press, 1964.

Morris, Joan. *The Lady Was a Bishop: The Hidden History of Women with Clerical Ordination and the Jurisdiction of Bishops.* New York: The Macmillan Company; London: Collier-Macmillan Limited, 1973.

Moulton, James Hope, "New Testament Greek in the Light of Modern Discovery," *Essays on Some Biblical Questions of the Day by Members of the University of Cambridge.* ed., Henry Barclay Swete. London: Macmillan and Co., Limited, 1909.

Payne, Robert. *The Horizon Book of Ancient Rome.* New York: American Heritage Publishing Co., Inc., 1966.

Peake, Arthur S. *A Critical Introduction to the New Testament.* New York: Charles Scribner's Sons, 1919.

----. *The Heroes and Martyrs of Faith (Studies in the Eleventh Chapter of the Epistle to the Hebrews).* London: Hodder and Stoughton, 1910.

Plumptre, E. H. "Aquila and Priscilla," *Biblical Studies.* London: Griffith, Farran, Okeden and Welch, 1885.

Poland, Franz, E. Reisinger and R. Wagner. *The Culture of Ancient Rome and Greece.* tr. John Henry Freese. London: George Harrap & Co., Ltd., 1926.

Prohl, Russell C. *Woman in the Church.* Grand Rapids: Wm. B. Eerdmans Publishing Company, 1957.

Ramsay, Sir Wm. M. *The Bearing of Recent Discoveries on the Trustworthiness of the New Testament.* London: Hodder & Stoughton, 1915.

----. *The Church in the Roman Empire Before A.D. 170.* London: Hodder & Stoughton, 1892.

----. *The Cities of St. Paul.* New York: A. D. Armstrong and Sons and London: Hodder & Stoughton, 1908.

Riddle, Donald Wayne. "Early Christian Hospitality: A Factor in the Gospel Tradition," *Journal of Biblical Literature* Vol. LVII. Philadelphia: Society of Biblical Literature, 1938.

Robertson, James Alex. *The Hidden Romance of the New Testament.* Boston: The Pilgrim Press; London: James Clarke & Co., Ltd., 1923.

Schiele, Friedrich Michael. "Harnack's 'Probabilia' Concerning the Address and Author of the Epistle to the Hebrews", *The American Journal of Theology*, 1905 (290-306).

Smalley, Stephen S. "Hebrews", *Exploring New Testament Backgrounds: a special survey of the New Testament books.* Presented by Christianity Today, n.d.

Smith, Paul R. *Is it Okay to Call God "Mother"?: Considering the Feminine Face of God.* Peabody, Mass: Hendrickson Publishers, 1993.

Starr, Lee Anna. *The Bible Status of Woman.* Zarephath, NJ: Pillar of Fire, 1955 (c. 1926 by Lee Anna Starr).

Tasker, R. V. G. "The Integrity of the Epistle to the Hebrews", *Expository Times* 47 (1935-36).

Thompson, J. A. *The Bible and Archeology.* Grand Rapids: Wm. B. Eerdmans Publishing Co., 1962.

Trudinger, L. Paul. "A Note on Heb. 13:22", *Journal of Theological Studies* 23 (1972).

Tuker, Mildred A. R. "The Gospel According to Prisca", *Nineteenth Century* 73 (1913).

VanDevelder, Frank R. *The Biblical Journey of Faith: The Road of the Sojourner.* Phil.: Fortress Press, 1988.

Verkuyl, G. "The Berkeley Version of the N.T.," BT 2 (1951). (*Bible Translator*).

Wegener, G.S. *6000 Years of the Bible.* tr., Margaret Shenfield. New York: Harper & Row, 1963.

Wikenhauser, Alfred. *New Testament Introduction.* tr., Joseph Cunningham. New York: Herder & Herder, Inc., 1958.

Wire, Antoinette Clark. *The Corinthian Women Prophets.* Minneapolis: Fortress Press, 1990.

Witherington, Ben III. *Women in the Earliest Churches.* Cambridge: University Press, 1988.

DEAD SEA SCROLLS

Allegro, John. *The Dead Sea Scrolls.* Baltimore: Penguin Books, Inc., 1956.

Burrows, Millar. *The Dead Sea Scrolls.* New York: The Viking Press, 1955; New York: Gramercy Publishing Co., 1986.

Brownlee, W. H. "John the Baptist in the New Light of Ancient Scrolls"; Raymond E. Brown, "The Qumran Scrolls and the Johannine Gospel and Epistles"; Karl Georg Kuhn, "The Two Messiahs of Aaron and Israel", *The Scrolls and the New Testament.* ed., Krister Stendahl. New York: Harper & Bros., 1957.

Cook, Edward M. *Solving the Mysteries of the Dead Sea Scrolls.* Grand Rapids: Zondervan Publishing House, 1994.

Daniélou, Jean. *The Dead Sea Scrolls and Primitive Christianity.* tr., Salvatore Attanasio. Baltimore: Helicon Press, Inc., 1958.

Spicq, Ceslas, *L'Epitre aux Hebreux* Vol. I. Paris: Gabalda, 1952.

Talmon, Shemaryahu, "Waiting for the Messiah: The Spiritual Universe of The Qumran Covenanters"; Macrae, George, S.J., "Messiah and Gospel", *Judaisms and Their Messiahs at the Turn of the Christian Era.* Cambridge: Cambridge University Press, 1987.

Vanderkam, James C., "Implications for the History of Judaism and Christianity," *The Dead Sea Scrolls After Forty Years.* Washington, DC: Biblical Archaeology Society, Symposium at the Smithsonian Institution Oct. 27, 1990, c. 1991, 1992.

Wise, Michael O. and Tabor, James D., "The Messiah at Qumran," *Biblical Archaeology Review* Vol. 18 No. 6, Nov/Dec 1992.

BIOGRAPHICAL

The Book of Saints. Comp. by the Benedictine monks of St. Augustine's Abbey, Ramsgate in Rome. 5th edition. New York: Thos. Crowell Co., 1966.

Butler's Lives of the Saints. Vol. III. Complete edition. ed., Herbert Thurston and Donald Attwater. New York: P. J. Kennedy & Sons, 1956.

Deen, Edith. *All of the Women of the Bible.* New York: Harper & Bros., Publishers, 1955.

Dictionnaire d'archeologie chretienne et de liturgie (DACL). Paris, 1940.

The Saints, A Concise Biographical Dictionary. ed., John Coulson. New York: Hawthorn Books Inc., 1958.

Hallett, Judith P. *Fathers and Daughters in Roman Society (Women and the Elite Family)*. Princeton, New Jersey: Princeton University Press, 1984.

Hertling, Ludwig and Englebert Kirschbaum. *The Roman Catacombs and Their Martyrs*. tr. M. Joseph Costelloe. U.S.: The Bruce Publishing Co., 1956. tr. from *Die Romischen Katakomben und ihre Martyrer* by arrangement with Verlag Herder, Wien. (1950).

Holzner, Joseph. *Paul of Tarsus*. tr. Frederic C. Eckhoff from *Paulus, sein Leben und seine Briefen*, published by Herder & Co., Freiburg in Breisgau. St. Louis, Mo., and London: Herder & Co., 1944.

Lockyer, Herbert. *All the Men of the Bible*. Grand Rapids: Zondervan Publishing Co., 1958.

Morton, H. V. *In the Steps of St. Paul*. 13th printing. New York: Dodd, Mead & Co., 1936.

Paulys Real-Encyclopadie der Classischen Altertumswissenschaft, Vol. I. Stuttgart: J. B. Metzlerscher Verlag, 1894. (Genealogical data about the Acilii Glabriones).

Price, Eugenia. *God Speaks to Women Today*. Grand Rapids: Zondervan Publishing Co., 1964.

Spence-Jones, H.D.M. *The Early Christians in Rome*. London: Methuen & Co., Ltd., 1910.

The Catholic Encyclopedia, Vol. VI and XII. New York: The Gilmary Soc., and The Encyclopedic Press Inc., 1913.

Tuker, M. A. R. and Hope Malleson. *Handbook to Christian and Ecclesiastical Rome, Part I, The Christian Monuments of Rome*. London: Adam and Charles Black, 1900.

Walsh, Wm. Thomas. *Saint Peter the Apostle*. New York: The Macmillan Co., 1948.

VATICAN CODEX

Vat. lat. 9698. Notice from Carrara to treasurer of Pope Pius VI about bronze plaque found at site of Priscilla's domicile.

INDEX OF NAMES